KU-203-013

Contents

Introduction

Biotechnology is Volume 281 in the **ISSUES** series. The aim of the series is to offer current, diverse information about important issues in our world, from a UK perspective.

ABOUT BIOTECHNOLOGY

Biotechnology is a topic that remains consistently controversial. This book explores the many issues and innovations surrounding the field, and considers its uses in both animal and plant sciences (e.g. synthetic milk or genetically modified crops). It also provides an overview of biotechnology as a whole.

OUR SOURCES

Titles in the **ISSUES** series are designed to function as educational resource books, providing a balanced overview of a specific subject.

The information in our books is comprised of facts, articles and opinions from many different sources, including:

⇨ Newspaper reports and opinion pieces

⇨ Website factsheets

⇨ Magazine and journal articles

⇨ Statistics and surveys

⇨ Government reports

⇨ Literature from special interest groups

A NOTE ON CRITICAL EVALUATION

Because the information reprinted here is from a number of different sources, readers should bear in mind the origin of the text and whether the source is likely to have a particular bias when presenting information (or when conducting their research). It is hoped that, as you read about the many aspects of the issues explored in this book, you will critically evaluate the information presented.

It is important that you decide whether you are being presented with facts or opinions. Does the writer give a biased or unbiased report? If an opinion is being expressed, do you agree with the writer? Is there potential bias to the 'facts' or statistics behind an article?

ASSIGNMENTS

In the back of this book, you will find a selection of assignments designed to help you engage with the articles you have been reading and to explore your own opinions. Some tasks will take longer than others and there is a mixture of design, writing and research-based activities that you can complete alone or in a group.

FURTHER RESEARCH

At the end of each article we have listed its source and a website that you can visit if you would like to conduct your own research. Please remember to critically evaluate any sources that you consult and consider whether the information you are viewing is accurate and unbiased.

Useful weblinks

www.animalaid.org.uk

www.bio.org

www.bch.cbd.int

www.edp24.co.uk

www.foe.co.uk

www.foe.org

www.genewatch.org

www.ibtimes.co.uk

www.independentsciencenews.org

www.labmate-online.com

www.littlegreenblog.com

www.monsantoblog.eu

www.mrc.ac.uk

www.ox.ac.uk

www.philiplymbery.com

www.shoutoutuk.org

www.stopthecrop.org

www.understandinganimalresearch.org.uk

ANDOVER COLLEGE

063300

Biotechnology

Series Editor: Cara Acred

Volume 281

Independence Educational Publishers

First published by Independence Educational Publishers

The Studio, High Green

Great Shelford

Cambridge CB22 5EG

England

© Independence 2015

Copyright

This book is sold subject to the condition that it shall not,
by way of trade or otherwise, be lent, resold, hired out or otherwise
circulated in any form of binding or cover other than that in which it
is published without the publisher's prior consent.

Photocopy licence

The material in this book is protected by copyright. However, the
purchaser is free to make multiple copies of particular articles for instructional
purposes for immediate use within the purchasing institution.
Making copies of the entire book is not permitted.

British Library Cataloguing in Publication Data

Biotechnology. -- (Issues ; 281)

1. Biotechnology--Moral and ethical aspects.

2. Biotechnology.

I. Series II. Acred, Cara editor.

174.9'6606-dc23

ISBN-13: 9781861687098

Printed in Great Britain

Zenith Print Group

Chapter 1

What is biotechnology?

What is biotechnology?

At its simplest, biotechnology is technology based on biology – biotechnology harnesses cellular and biomolecular processes to develop technologies and products that help improve our lives and the health of our planet. We have used the biological processes of microorganisms for more than 6,000 years to make useful food products, such as bread and cheese, and to preserve dairy products.

Modern biotechnology provides breakthrough products and technologies to combat debilitating and rare diseases, reduce our environmental footprint, feed the hungry, use less and cleaner energy, and have safer, cleaner and more efficient industrial manufacturing processes.

Currently, there are more than 250 biotechnology healthcare products and vaccines available to patients, many for previously untreatable diseases. More than 18 million farmers around the world use agricultural biotechnology to increase yields, prevent damage from insects and pests and reduce farming's impact on the environment. And more than 50 biorefineries are being built across North America to test and refine technologies to produce biofuels and chemicals from renewable biomass, which can help reduce greenhouse gas emissions.

Recent advances in biotechnology are helping us prepare for and meet society's most pressing challenges. Here's how:

Heal the world

Biotech is helping to heal the world by harnessing nature's own toolbox and using our own genetic make-up to heal and guide lines of research by:

⇨ Reducing rates of infectious disease;

⇨ Saving millions of children's lives;

⇨ Changing the odds of serious, life-threatening conditions affecting millions around the world;

⇨ Tailoring treatments to individuals to minimise health risks and side effects;

⇨ Creating more precise tools for disease detection; and

⇨ Combating serious illnesses and everyday threats confronting the developing world.

Fuel the world

Biotech uses biological processes such as fermentation and harnesses biocatalysts such as enzymes, yeast and other microbes to become microscopic manufacturing plants. Biotech is helping to fuel the world by:

⇨ Streamlining the steps in chemical manufacturing processes by 80% or more;

⇨ Lowering the temperature for cleaning clothes and potentially saving $4.1 billion annually;

⇨ Improving manufacturing process efficiency to save 50% or more on operating costs;

⇨ Reducing use of and reliance on petrochemicals;

⇨ Using biofuels to cut greenhouse gas emissions by 52% or more;

⇨ Decreasing water usage and waste generation; and

⇨ Tapping into the full potential of traditional biomass waste products.

Feed the world

Biotech improves crop insect resistance, enhances crop herbicide tolerance and facilitates the use of more environmentally sustainable farming practices. Biotech is helping to feed the world by:

⇨ Generating higher crop yields with fewer inputs;

⇨ Lowering volumes of agricultural chemicals required by crops – limiting the run-off of these products into the environment;

⇨ Using biotech crops that need fewer applications of pesticides and that allow farmers to reduce tilling farmland;

⇨ Developing crops with enhanced nutrition profiles that solve vitamin and nutrient deficiencies;

⇨ Producing foods free of allergens and toxins such as mycotoxin; and

⇨ Improving food and crop oil content to help improve cardiovascular health.

⇨ The above information is reprinted with kind permission from the Biotechnology Industry Organization. Please visit www.bio.org for further information.

© Biotechnology Industry Organization 2015

Biosafety and biotechnology

1. What is biotechnology?

The term 'biotechnology' refers to any technological application that uses biological systems, living organisms, or derivatives thereof, to make or modify products or processes for a specific use.

Biotechnology, in the form of traditional fermentation techniques, has been used for decades to make bread, cheese or beer. It has also been the basis of traditional animal and plant breeding techniques, such as hybridisation and the selection of plants and animals with specific characteristics to create, for example, crops which produce higher yields of grain.

The difference with modern biotechnology is that researchers can now take a single gene from a plant or animal cell and insert it in another plant or animal cell to give it a desired characteristic, such as a plant that is resistant to a specific pest or disease.

In the Biosafety Protocol, modern biotechnology means the application of:

⇨ *In vitro* nucleic acid techniques, including recombinant deoxyribonucleic acid (DNA) and direct injection of nucleic acid into cells or organelles, or

⇨ Fusion of cells beyond the taxonomic family, that overcome natural physiological reproductive or recombination barriers and that are not techniques used in traditional breeding and selection.

2. What is biosafety?

Biosafety is a term used to describe efforts to reduce and eliminate the potential risks resulting from biotechnology and its products. For the purposes of the Biosafety Protocol, this is based on the precautionary approach, whereby the lack of full scientific certainty should not be used as an excuse to postpone action when there is a threat of serious or irreversible damage. While developed countries that are at the centre of the global biotechnology industry have established domestic biosafety regimes, many developing countries are only now starting to establish their own national systems.

3. What is a Living Modified Organism (LMO)?

A Living Modified Organism (LMO) is defined in the Cartagena Protocol on Biosafety as any living organism that possesses a novel combination of genetic material obtained through the use of modern biotechnology. The Protocol also defines the terms 'living organism' and 'modern biotechnology'. In everyday usage LMOs are usually considered to be the same as GMOs (Genetically Modified Organisms), but definitions and interpretations of the term GMO vary widely.

Common LMOs include agricultural crops that have been genetically modified for greater productivity or for resistance to pests or diseases. Examples of modified crops include tomatoes, cassava, corn, cotton and soybeans.

4. What are LMO products?

LMOs form the basis of a range of products and agricultural commodities. Processed products containing dead modified organisms or non-living GMO components include certain vaccines; drugs; food additives; and many processed, canned and preserved foods. They can also include corn and soybean derivatives used in many foods and non-foods, cornstarch used for cardboard and adhesives, fuel ethanol for gasoline, vitamins, vaccines and pharmaceuticals, and yeast-based foods such as beer and bread.

5. What are some potential benefits of biotechnology?

Genetic engineering promises remarkable advances in medicine, agriculture and other fields. These may include new medical treatments and vaccines, new industrial products, and improved fibres and fuels. Proponents of the technology argue that biotechnology has the potential to lead to increases in food security, decreased pressure on land use, sustainable yield increase in marginal lands or inhospitable environments and reduced use of water and agrochemicals in agriculture.

6. What are some potential risks of biotechnology?

Biotechnology is a very new field, and much about the interaction of LMOs with various ecosystems is not yet known. Some of the concerns about the new technology include its potential adverse effects on biological diversity, and potential risks to human health. Potential areas of concern might be unintended changes in the competitiveness, virulence, or other characteristics of the target species; the possibility of adverse impacts on non-target species (such as beneficial insects) and ecosystems; the potential for weediness in genetically modified crops (where a plant becomes more invasive than the original, perhaps by transferring its genes to wild relatives); and the stability of inserted genes (the possibilities that a gene will lose its effectiveness or will be re-transferred to another host).

7. Why do we need an international biosafety agreement?

While advances in biotechnology have great potential for significant improvements in human well-being, they must be developed and used with adequate safety measures for the environment and human health.

The objectives of the 1992 Convention on Biological Diversity are 'the conservation of biological diversity, the sustainable use of its components and the fair and equitable sharing of the benefits arising out of the utilization of genetic resources'. When developing the Convention, the negotiators recognised that biotechnology can make a contribution towards achieving the objectives of the Convention, if developed and used with adequate safety measures for the environment and human health. The Contracting Parties agreed to consider the need to develop appropriate procedures to address the safe transfer, handling and use of any LMO resulting from biotechnology that may have adverse effect on the conservation and sustainable use of biological diversity. The Biosafety Protocol is the result of that process.

⇨ The above information is reprinted with kind permission from the Secretariat of the Convention on Biological Diversity. Please visit www.bch.cbd.int for further information.

© SCBD 2001-2015

Synthetic biology: GMOs 2.0

What is synthetic biology?

Synthetic biology (synbio) is an extreme version of genetic engineering. Instead of swapping genes from one species to another (as in conventional genetic engineering), synthetic biologists employ a number of new genetic engineering techniques, such as using synthetic (human-made) DNA to create entirely new forms of life or to 'reprogramme' existing organisms to produce chemicals that they would not produce naturally.

Commercial use of synthetic biology: Is it 'natural', 'sustainable' or necessary?

In the absence of regulations to protect human health and the environment, and labelling to ensure consumer right-to-know, synthetic biology is about to enter the market via new ingredients for food, cosmetics and household products, many of which are being marketed as 'natural' and 'sustainable'. These new ingredients, including synbio versions of vanilla, stevia and saffron flavourings for food and beverages, and ingredients for cosmetics and cleaning products, are produced by synthetically engineered organisms, including synbio yeast and algae that are raised in vats and feed on sugar. The claims of 'sustainability' for this technology are questionable at best. While the industry claims that synthetic biology could reduce impacts on land by producing products in labs rather than in farm fields, currently commercialised artificial organisms (synbio yeast and algae) require sugar as a feedstock to live and reproduce. Expanding sugarcane plantations to meet feedstock demand from a growing synbio industry could exacerbate the current destruction of critical ecosystems in Latin America (including some of Brazil's most eco-sensitive land), Africa and Southeast Asia.[1] Commodities currently produced by small farmers (e.g. vanilla) may be displaced in favour of synthetic biology products, and the land they preserve (e.g. rain forests where vanilla beans are grown) may in turn be converted into industrial-scale plantations for soy, beef or sugar.

Risk of environmental escape and contamination

No containment strategies are foolproof, and we don't know how these organisms will interact with the environment. While some types of pollution can be cleaned up, synbio organisms are living and self-replicate. Once in the environment they may be impossible to recall or clean up.

Synthetic biology is virtually unregulated

Before synthetic biology ingredients get passed off as 'sustainable' or 'natural' or enter our food and consumer products, we need mandatory safety assessment and oversight specific to synthetic biology and the novel risks it may pose to our health and environment[2] to ensure these new genetically engineered organisms, and their products, are safe and sustainable.

In food: synbio vanilla flavouring

Real natural vanilla production can be environmentally sustainable, culturally critical and provides a livelihood for an estimated 200,000 small farmers. It is primarily grown and harvested by hand in intact rainforests in Madagascar and Mexico, helping to preserve rain forest ecosystems.[3] Synbio vanilla could be the most high-profile synbio ingredient to enter the market, will likely be unlabelled, and is currently marketed as 'natural'. Evolva, the synbio company that is preparing to launch this product this year, could capture a large percentage of the global vanilla flavour market. Since this product could be labelled as 'natural', food and consumer products companies could easily replace truly natural vanilla produced by small farmers with Evolva's 'natural' synbio vanilla, confusing consumers and harming small vanilla farmers across the global south.

'Synthetic biologists employ a number of new genetic engineering techniques, such as using synthetic (human-made) DNA to create entirely new forms of life or to "reprogramme" existing organisms to produce chemicals that they would not produce naturally'

In cosmetics: synbio squalane

Cosmetic products on the shelves may already include a synbio ingredient.[4] Amyris Biotechnologies produces synbio squalane used in an estimated 300 products, most of which are undisclosed. Squalane is currently primarily sourced from olive oil. A synbio company called Solazyme is developing a cocoa butter-like replacement for use in body care products, made from engineered algae.[5] However, consistent with the industry trend of little to no transparency, Solazyme does not disclose what specific genetic engineering techniques it uses to produce its oils.

In household products: synbio algal oil

In this process, engineered algae is fed sugar and excretes an oil high in fatty acids such as lauric and myristic acid, key compounds found naturally in palm kernel and coconut oils. Solazyme, this product's manufacturer, claims its algal oil may be replace unsustainable palm kernel oil.[6] However, synbio algal oil will more likely displace lauric oils on the market such as coconut oil and babaçu oil. Sustainably produced coconut oil is an example of a less risky, more sustainable and natural substitute for palm oil. Consumer products companies currently using or planning to use synbio ingredients include Ecover (parent company of Method), Unilever and Procter & Gamble.

For more information on synthetic biology, see www.foe.org/synbio, www.synbiowatch.org.

References

1. Mendonca, Maria Luisa. 'Brazil: sugar cane plantations devastate vital Cerrado region.' Pacific Ecologist 17 (2009): 25+. Academic OneFile. Web. 18 August 2014.

2. Drinkwater, Kelly, Todd Kuiken, Ph.D, Shlomiya Lightfoot, Julie McNamara, and Kenneth Oye, Ph.D. Creating a Research Agenda for the Ecological Implications of Synthetic Biology. Rep. Woodrow Wilson International Center for Scholars, May 2014. Web.

3. Communication with Michel Grisoni, CIRAD (Centre de cooperation internationale en recherché agronomique pour le developpement), based in Réunion. Vanilla production estimates provided by Michel Grisoni.

4. Strom, Stephanie. 'Companies Quietly Apply Biofuel Tools to Household Products.' The New York Times, 30 May 2014. Web.

5. Solazyme. www.solazyme.com/innovation.

6. Strom, Stephanie. 'Companies Quietly Apply Biofuel Tools to Household Products'.

⇨ The above information is reprinted with kind permission from Friends of the Earth U.S. Please visit www.foe.org for further information. The most recent version of the factsheet can be viewed here: http://webiva-downton.s3.amazonaws.com/877/88/b/5292/Issue_brief_-_Synbio_GMOs_2_2015.pdf

© Friends of the Earth U.S. 2015

Synthetic biology ingredients for food and cosmetics

On the market:

- Grapefruit flavouring
- Orange flavouring
- Resveratrol
- Patchouli
- Squalane (Neossance)
- Vetiver oil (vetivone, Epivone)

In the pipeline:

- Vanilla
- Stevia
- Saffron
- Cocoa butter
- Milk and egg substitutes
- Agarwood

A CRISPR future for genetic modification

Dr Ian Le Guillou looks at the impact of the new CRISPR technique for genetically modifying animals.

By Ian Le Guillou

The number of animal experiments in Britain has been increasing over the past 20 years. Looking at the statistics, there is one very clear reason why: breeding genetically modified mice. Breeding now accounts for over half of the animal experiments in Britain, compared to just 7% 20 years ago. In fact, without the animals used for breeding, the numbers of animal experiments has fallen by 600,000 since 1993.

So why do we have so many animals used for breeding? Improvements in our understanding of genetics and our technology have brought about a genetic revolution. The ability to genetically alter animals allows researchers to study diseases and conditions in a way that is much more relevant to patients. This can be as simple as studying the effects of removing a certain gene so that its role in a disease can be confirmed, or inserting a human gene in a mouse to study how a virus attacks our bodies.

The extra precision and relevance of studying genetically modified animals allows researchers to use fewer and less sentient animals. As I discussed in my last blog post, genetically modified mice can now replace the need for monkeys when testing the polio vaccine.

However, this has come at the cost of the millions of additional animals used for breeding. For the past few decades, our technique for creating genetically modified animals has been technically challenging. It involves inserting or removing genes in embryonic stem cells that are then injected into an early-stage mouse embryo. This results in a chimeric mouse that has only some cells that are genetically altered. Researchers then have to check if the altered gene can be passed on to any of its offspring. These offspring then need to be cross-bred to create mice that

have two copies of the gene. At every step along this way there are multiple mice that do not carry the gene or cannot pass the gene on, all of which are of limited use to researchers.

A new way of modifying DNA, known as CRISPR, can reduce much of this breeding. CRISPR was discovered in the primitive immune system of bacteria, and it has some very useful features. It enables researchers to create a break in the DNA helix at very specific places, where they can then introduce mutations as the break is repaired.

This level of precision can be applied to single-celled embryos in the very early stage of development and avoids many of the multiple steps for creating genetically modified animals: several genes can be edited at once, both copies of the gene can be changed and there is no need for a supply of embryonic stem cells.

The CRISPR system was first developed in 2012 and there has been a significant buzz about it in the scientific community. The precision offered by this technique offers an additional level of refinement for researchers – if they can produce better, more faithful, models for diseases then the results will be even more reliable.

The technique is still in its infancy and researchers are still checking for unintended effects and finding new ways of applying it to difficult problems. The potential for CRISPR is massive. It is cheaper, simpler, more reliable, and requires fewer animals. This powerful combination offers scientists the opportunity to make huge leaps in our understanding of genetics, improve models of human diseases, and ultimately develop new treatments and cures.

29 July 2014

⇨ The above information is reprinted with kind permission from Understanding Animal Research. Please visit www.understandinganimalresearch.org.uk for further information.

© *Understanding Animal Research 2015*

Norfolk MP says EU's hostility towards science is hampering investment

The rise of an 'increasingly science hostile' European Union is undermining our attractiveness as a place to invest, MP George Freeman has said while calling for reform or the UK would try to 'take back' science regulation from Brussels.

By Annabelle Dickson

The Norfolk MP will today publish a report for the European reform project, Fresh Start, in which he highlights an increasing tide of 'anti-biotech' legislation.

He said the EU's hostility to Genetically Modified crops had already seen German based BASF and US major Monsanto announcing its withdrawal from Europe in agricultural research and development, adding that the EU policy-making machine was being driven by 'increasingly strident and politically active biotech-hostile lobbying groups, and minority political parties exercising influence through the coalition politics of member states'.

Mr Freeman said the Norwich Research Park and 'Norfolk-Cambridge corridor' was an opportunity to attract major inward investment, but the opportunities could be put at risk by EU legislation.

He said: 'Increasingly institutionalised prejudice against the appliance of science and biotechnology in key sectors of medicine and food and agriculture risks condemning Europe to a new 'dark age', cut off from playing a potentially major role pioneering the new technologies with the potential to help feed, fuel and heal the developing world, tackling the growing global crisis of food and medicine.

'Over the next 30 years the world faces a major Global Challenge in the three core life science sectors of food, medicine and energy: how to double world food production to feed nine billion people in 2050, with half as much water and energy, from the same land mass?

'Biotechnology is the defining technology of our age, with technologies such as GM, nanotech and genomic medicine unlocking new opportunities for the world's population to transform the life prospects of the poorest people on Earth.

'But the rise of an increasingly science hostile green politics in Europe is starting to undermine Europe's attractiveness as a location for biotech investment, and risks condemning Europe as a backwater in some of the most exciting fields of human endeavour.'

10 January 2014

⇨ The above information is reprinted with kind permission from *Eastern Daily Press*. Please visit www.edp24.co.uk for further information.

© 2015 Archant Community Media Ltd

Public Attitudes to Science 2014

Public Attitudes to Science (PAS) 2014 is the fifth in a series of studies looking at attitudes to science, scientists and science policy among the UK public.

51% Half say they hear and see too little about science.

75% Three-quarters think that 'the Government should act in accordance with public concerns about science and technology'.

People are now more comfortable about the pace of change – just a third now agree that 'science makes people's lives change too fast'. **34%** (49% in 1988)

More now agree that 'it is important to know about science in my daily life' **72%** (57% in 1988)

69% Seven-in-ten think that 'scientists should listen more to what ordinary people think'.

Source: Ipsos MORI, 14 March 2014 (fieldwork: 15 July – 18 November 2013), *Public Attitudes to Science 2014*

World's first artificial enzymes created using synthetic biology

Medical Research Council (MRC) scientists have created the world's first enzymes made from artificial genetic material. Their synthetic enzymes, which are made from molecules that do not occur anywhere in nature, are capable of triggering chemical reactions in the lab.

The research, published today in *Nature*, gives new insights into the origins of life and could provide a starting point for an entirely new generation of drugs and diagnostics.

The findings build on previous work by the team at the MRC Laboratory of Molecular Biology, which saw them create synthetic molecules called 'XNAs' that can store and pass on genetic information, in a similar way to DNA.

Using their lab-made XNAs as building blocks, the team has now created 'XNAzymes', which power simple reactions, such as cutting up or stitching together small chunks of RNA, just like naturally occurring enzymes.

Dr Philipp Holliger, who led the research at the MRC Laboratory of Molecular Biology, said:

'All life on Earth depends on a series of chemical reactions, from digesting food to making DNA in our cells. Many of these reactions are too sluggish to happen at ambient temperatures and pressures, and require enzymes to kick-start or 'catalyse' the process.'

Every one of our cells contains thousands of different enzymes, many of which are proteins. But some of the key fundamental reactions necessary for life are performed by RNA, a close chemical cousin of DNA. Life itself is thought to have begun with the evolution of a self-copying RNA enzyme.

Dr Holliger explains: 'Until recently, it was thought that DNA and RNA were the only molecules that could store genetic information and, together with proteins, the only biomolecules able to form enzymes. Our work suggests that, in principle, there are a number of possible alternatives to nature's molecules that will support the catalytic processes required for life. Life's 'choice' of RNA and DNA may just be an accident of prehistoric chemistry.'

Dr Alex Taylor, the study's first author in Phil Holliger's lab at the MRC Laboratory of Molecular Biology, and a Post-doctoral Research Associate at St John's College, Cambridge, adds: 'The creation of synthetic DNA, and now enzymes, from building blocks that don't exist in nature also raises the possibility that, if there is life on other planets, it may have sprung up from an entirely different set of molecules, and it widens the possible number of planets that might be able to host life.'

DNA and RNA are the building blocks of life, storing all of our genetic information and passing it on to future generations.

In 2012, Dr Holliger's group showed that six alternative molecules, called XNAs, could also store genetic information and evolve through natural selection. They have now expanded on this principle to discover, for the first time, four different types of synthetic catalyst formed from these entirely unnatural building blocks.

The XNAzymes are capable of catalysing simple reactions like cutting and joining RNA strands in a test tube. One of the XNAzymes can even join XNA strands together, which represents one of the first steps to creating a living system.

Because their XNAzymes are much more stable than naturally occurring enzymes, the scientists believe they could be particularly useful in developing new therapies for a range of diseases, including cancers and viral infections, which exploit the body's natural processes to take hold in the body.

Dr Holliger added: 'Our XNAs are chemically extremely robust and, because they do not occur in nature, they are not recognised by the body's natural degrading enzymes. This might make them an attractive candidate for long-lasting treatments that can disrupt disease-related RNAs.'

Professor Patrick Maxwell, Chair of the MRC's Molecular and Cellular Medicine Board, said:

'Synthetic biology is delivering some truly amazing advances that promise to change the way we understand and treat disease. The UK excels in this field, and this latest advance offers the tantalising prospect of using designer biological parts as a starting point for an entirely new class of therapies and diagnostic tools that are more effective and have a longer shelf-life.'

Funders of this work included the MRC, European Science Foundation and the Biotechnology and Biological Sciences Research Council.

1 December 2014

⇨ The above information is reprinted with kind permission from Medical Research Council. Please visit www.mrc.ac.uk for further information.

© *Medical Research Council 2015*

Designer viruses could be the new antibiotics

An article from The Conversation.

By Luc Henry, Postdoctoral Fellow at Swiss Federal Institute of Technology in Lausanne

THE CONVERSATION

Bacterial infections remain a major threat to human and animal health. Worse still, the catalogue of useful antibiotics is shrinking as pathogens build up resistance to these drugs. There are a few promising new drugs in the pipeline, but they may not prove to be enough. Multi-resistant organisms – also called 'superbugs' – are on the rise and many predict a gloomy future if nothing is done to fight back.

The answer, some believe, may lie in using engineered bacteriophages – types of viruses that infects bacteria. Two recent studies, both published in the journal *Nature Biotechnology*, show a promising alternative to small-molecule drugs that are the mainstay of antibiotics today.

From basic to synthetic biology

Every living organism has evolved simple mechanisms to protect itself from harmful pathogens. This innate immune system can be a passive barrier, blocking anything above a certain size, or an active response that recognises foreign molecules – such as proteins and DNA – then kills them.

In bacteria, an important component of the immune system is composed of a family of proteins, which is tasked specifically with breaking down foreign DNA. Each bug produces a set of these proteins that chew the genetic material of viruses and other micro-organisms into pieces while leaving its own genome intact.

In vertebrates, a more advanced mechanism – called the adaptive immune system – creates a molecular memory of previous attacks and prepares the organism for the next wave of infection. This is the principle on which vaccines are built. Upon introduction of harmless pathogen fragments, the adaptive immunity will train specialist killer cells that later allow a faster and more specific response upon contact with the virulent agent.

Crisp news

Until recently, people thought bacteria were too simple to possess any sort of adaptive immunity. But in 2007 a group of scientists from the dairy industry showed that bacteria commonly used for the production of cheese and yogurts could be 'vaccinated' by exposure to a virus. Two years earlier, others had noticed similarities between repetitive sections in bacterial genomes and the DNA of viruses. These repetitive sequences – called CRISPR for 'clustered regularly interspaced short palindromic repeats' – had been known for 20 years but no one could ever explain their function.

With both these observations it quickly became clear that bacteria were introducing viral DNA fragments into their own genome to protect themselves from later attacks. But it took another five years to get the whole picture.

In 2012, a German team identified all the pieces and showed how exactly bacteria transcribe viral DNA into a short RNA – usually the messenger molecule – which guides the DNA-cutting protein called Cas9 and tells it where to chop off viral DNA.

This could have been just one more interesting scientific observation, but in an era of synthetic biology, natural functions can quickly become designers' tools. Within two years, many laboratories demonstrated that, by tailoring the short RNA guide, any gene could be cut out from a chromosome using the CRISPR-Cas9 system.

Since that breakthrough, hundreds of scientists have used it to manipulate the genome of bacteria, yeast, worms, crops, fruit flies, zebrafish, mice, rats or even human cells. Although there are limitations, a procedure that used to take months using previous technologies – such as breeding or genome editing – can now be done in a few weeks.

Bacterial immunity, rewired

Now two teams of scientists, one led by Timothy Lu of the Massachusetts Institute of Technology and the other by Luciano Marriffini of Rockefeller University, each used the CRISPR-Cas9 system to generate their own version of a prototype technology that turns a bacteria's defence mechanism into a self-destructing weapon. The main idea behind their work was to use genetic engineering to rewire the bacteria's immunity to produce 'boomerang antibiotics that target' only bugs carrying specific genes.

To do this, their teams built an artificial CRISPR-Cas9 system – that could cut out specific genes – by assembling pieces in the lab before reintroducing it back into bacteria using viruses. Once injected into the bug, the guide RNA recruits the Cas9 protein to target genes that endow the bug antibiotic resistance or other harmful properties by embedding viral DNA. After those genes are removed, the superbug either dies or turns into a harmless one.

Although the method still needs improving to become useful for treatment, its ability to specifically kill pathogens has significant potential because it can limit their spread to other bacteria.

Fighting antibiotic resistance would not be the only application for these engineered viruses. Current small-molecule antibiotics also end up killing other healthy bacteria in our body. The new method would the harmless bugs intact, and thus minimise side-effects of antibiotics use.

In the past few years, the role of friendly microbes living in the human gut has become clearer. Imbalance in the diversity of species and their relative abundance may influence the development of certain conditions – including depression, diabetes and obesity. In this context, engineered viruses that would restore or shape the microbiota (or flora) could greatly improve health.

14 October 2014

⇨ The above information is reprinted with kind permission from The Conversation. Please visit www.theconversation.com for further information.

© 2010–2015,
The Conversation Trust (UK)

How to unboil an egg method developed by University of California, Irvine scientists

By Ryan Barrell

A radical breakthrough by University of California, Irvine scientists has developed a method to reverse the cooking process of a hen's egg.

Seemingly pointless, the technique could actually lead to a significant reduction in the cost of cancer treatments.

It may also help cheese production and could have applications in the biotechnology industry.

When the egg is cooked, long strands of amino acids become tangled. Attempting to untangle them is a very difficult process, but the new technique produced by UC Irvine takes just minutes.

The eggs used weren't simply hard boiled, they were cooked for 20 minutes at 90 degrees Celsius, but this can be undone with the addition of urea.

Urea is a main component of urine, and can turn boiled egg whites into liquid. The amino acids are then untangled using a vortex fluid device consisting of a thin glass tube spun at 5,000 rpm.

One of the main applications for the research would be to produce cheaper cancer antibodies, which are currently made using expensive hamster ovaries. This new method of unboiling may allow them to produce in much cheaper yeast or bacteria cells.

28 January 2015

⇨ The above information is reprinted with kind permission from The Huffington Post UK. Please visit www.huffingtonpost.co.uk for further information.

© 2015 AOL (UK) Limited

Three-parent babies: a step too far?

Science, especially the field of genetic engineering, has been a controversial topic for decades. The question, 'when does this become 'playing God'?' is frequently asked. Where do we draw the line? Well, apparently not at three-parent babies.

By Christina Kassab

The research for three-parent babies has been around for a while. The babies would have three genetic parents, created through a specialised form of *in vitro* fertilisation. The procedure is intended to prevent mitochondrial diseases including diabetes mellitus and deafness and some heart and liver conditions. In 2000, a girl in the US (Alana Saarinen) was conceived through an infertility treatment known as cytoplasmic transfer and has DNA from three biological parents. As a result of this, several research teams in the United Kingdom requested a regulatory approval for a similar technique called mitochondrial replacement. In February 2015, the House of Lords legalised three-parent babies.

Professor Dagan Wells, Associate Professor at the NIHR Biomedical Research Centre, University of Oxford argues:

'Disorders involving defective mitochondria can have catastrophic consequences for the affected individuals, sometimes causing death during infancy. For many years it has been possible to diagnose mitochondrial conditions, but what then? There have been few treatment options and no cure.

'Now, after years of careful research, we are finally at a point where a cure for mitochondrial disorders may be within reach. There has been an opportunity for public consultation and this has revealed broad support for the use of this therapy under appropriate regulation. The most telling thing is the support for mitochondrial donation from affected families.

'None of us can understand the impact of a mitochondrial disorder as well as they do, so their voices need to be heard. The way in which rigorous scientific research and vigorous public debate have been carried out in parallel in this instance will serve as a model for how ethically challenging scientific advances should be considered for clinical use in the future.'

Children born from mothers who carry faulty mitochondria can be healthy and free from deadly conditions caused by serious mitochondrial disease. If we can prevent suffering from disease we cannot control, is it not our responsibility to prevent it? Is this not the right thing to do?

Although this technique could reduce the amount of babies born with health problems, there are many ethical issues surrounding the procedure.

Embryos in this procedure will also have to be created simply in order to be destroyed. These embryos have the potential to become a human life, do they then not deserve the same rights as everyone else? Is it morally right, to experiment on them? Shinya Yamanaka, a Nobel Prize-winning stem cell researcher once said, 'When I saw the embryo, I suddenly realised there was such a small difference between it and my daughters. I thought, we can't keep destroying embryos for our research. There must be another way.'

Some people are troubled by the fact that these procedures could have psychological and emotional impacts on a child's life, especially that child's sense of identity. When it comes to mitochondrial transfer, 'second mothers' will remain anonymous, under the draft regulations. Doesn't a child have the right to know their parentage? Do they not have the right to know their true identities? If a third party has contributed DNA, are they not in fact a parent? Why should they not have a say in the child's life? Who are the real parents?

These treatments could alter genes across generations, although this has not been proven, while the safety and efficacy of mitochondrial DNA replacement remains unanswered. The World Health Organization says that techniques 'where there is an intention or possibility of altering genes passed on to the next generation... should not be permitted in the foreseeable future'. Long-term side effects are unknown, so is this a risk that we should be willing to take?

Opponents to three-parent babies argue that scientists are 'playing God'. Do we have the right to change the genes of generations to come without knowing the implications? If we can conceive three-parent babies, what is to stop people from choosing the colour of their children's eyes? Their hair colour? This could mean that there will be a sharp decline in the amount of disabled in society. Does this mean that they are somehow lesser people than everyone else? Are 'designer babies' an option we really want to allow in the future?

Whether you believe that mitochondrial treatment is a step in the right or the wrong direction, there are implications to this technique that have to be seriously considered. The UK has already legalised this procedure but is it the right decision? Is this a step too far?

12 March 2015

⇨ The above information is reprinted with kind permission from Shout Out UK. Please visit www.shoutoutuk.org for further information.

© Shout Out UK 2015

Meet the Transhumanist Party: 'Want to live forever? Vote for me'

Jamie Bartlett meets Zoltan Istvan, the man behind a political movement in America that wants to make us all more than human.

By Jamie Bartlett

It usually takes a lifetime for a radical political movement to graduate from the margins to the mainstream. That's okay, since Zoltan Istvan is planning to live 10,000 years. Zoltan, whom I've profiled here, is a transhumanist.

Transhumanists, broadly speaking, are people who want us to become 'beyond human'. It's an umbrella term for a broad family of ideas united by the vision that technology now, or at least soon will, allow us to greatly enhance human intellectual, physical, and psychological capacities. That means everything from bionic limbs to 3D printing organs to uploading our entire brains on to memory sticks and carrying them around with us as back up.

But ideas are not enough for this fledgling movement. Transhumanism remains a smallish but well-funded movement – Humanity+, the largest formal umbrella group, has just under 10,000 members from around the world, and they are largely rich Californians, technology geeks and scientists (sometimes all three). And it remains mostly confined to the West. That's why, in October this year, Zoltan decided to form the Transhumanist Party, and run for president in the 2016 US presidential election.

As you might have guessed, Zoltan will be running on a pretty interesting policy platform. First up – and a particular interest of Zoltan's, who I've come to believe is genuinely determined to live forever – is life extension. This is the study of keeping people alive for as long as possible, either by slowing the ageing process or extending lifespan. 'Few fields of study offer so much for civilisation,' Zoltan tells me. 'And we're not far off the science being available so people can start living a lot longer – maybe even 50 years or 100 years in the very near future'. I'm not sure how accurate his timelines are – others in the Transhumanist movement are a little more cautious. But as it stands he reckons there's hardly any investment in research of this type – about $1 billion a year (and most of this is on diseases like Alzheimer's and Parkinson's). In terms of what Zoltan considers life extension science – stopping ageing and eliminating death entirely – it's far, far less. Because of that Zoltan thinks we're letting people die unnecessarily. In a tidy populist touch, he plans to significantly curtail military spending in favour of research into all this. With enough resources, he thinks we can 'conquer' ageing within a decade. The Transhumanist Party advocates spending at least a trillion dollars over ten years directly on life extension research.

Then there's perhaps the most important policy of all: how to manage the existential risks of rapid scientific advance: engineered viruses, nano-technology, home-made bio-hacking, and of course, artificial intelligence. Ray Kurzweil – probably the world's most famous Transhumanist, who works for Google – thinks 'the singularity' (the point at which artificial intelligence becomes so smart that it starts making even smarter versions of itself, leaving us mortals trailing behind) will be with us in 2045. It's a terrifying prospect. The Transhumanists themselves seem divided, although most agree that it's at least a possibility this century. No party, argues Zoltan, is thinking properly about any of this, but they could become major threats to civilisation in the near future. 'I'm not entirely sure yet how we'd regulate it, but the Transhumanist Party will make this a top priority,' he explains. 'Of course I support AI, nano-technology and other radical engineering, and would increase funding for all of it significant, but strict safeguards need to be in place too.'

Zoltan also wants to make college mandatory, and free, for everyone. Which in fact sounds rather good. 'If we all live to 140, we're going to need a smarter, more capable population', he explains, when I suggest it sounds a bit Scandinavian for a Californian-based party that has tones of libertarianism. Of course, the Transhumanist Party doesn't yet have thought through policies on the bread and butter of government: immigration, housing policy, social welfare, and so on. Not that it matters, since at this point Zoltan doesn't

> **Transhumanists [...] are people who want us to become 'beyond human'. It's an umbrella term for a broad family of ideas united by the vision that technology now, or at least soon will, allow us to greatly enhance human intellectual, physical, and psychological capacities.**

really intend to win – rather raise awareness about the party and the movement. Running for President will give him a platform, he hopes, to demonstrate that science and technology is good for people, for health and for wellbeing. (Interestingly, Zoltan thinks that his main adversaries in the future will be religious groups).

So what are his chances? It's true we're living in an age of political radicalism, and Zoltan hopes to capitalise on the frustration with centre-Left and Right 'establishment' parties. Across Europe and the US the share of the vote among the big mainstream parties has been falling for years, with the leftovers being picked off by Tea Partyers, Ukippers, the Five Star Movement, and so on. 'I realise I won't win it this time around,' he tells me. 'But by 2024 we will be a real, legitimate party with likely over half a million members – approaching the Greens or the Libertarians. That's when we'll really make our move.'

I think he's right that there will be space in politics for a movement that addresses our relationship with technology explicitly. I'm not sure how accurate his timeline is (scientists I've spoken to are more sceptical), but it's certainly true that there are mind-boggling things under way. At Chalmers University of Technology in Sweden, scientists are already connecting robotic limbs to the human nervous system of amputees: the first arm surgeries are scheduled to occur in less than 12 months. Then there's the 'Iron Man' armour suit being created for American soldiers. Panasonic will be releasing an exoskeleton suit shortly. Injectable oxygen shots are already here. Some video games are already being played via mind-reading helmets. Enhanced contact lenses will soon allow people to have infrared night vision. It does all throw up important ethical and philosophical challenges. Is an uploaded mind still human? Should we give 'human rights' to an artificial intelligence with a superior intellect to a human? Then there's the social problems.

Presumably, human enhancement technologies would be disproportionately available to those with greater financial resources, creating a genetic divide. And if you lived forever, are you taking up the place of another generation? What about the more mundane things: what would be a fair prison sentence for murder if we could all live for 200 years? Or the right retirement age. I'm guessing it won't be 70 if we can all make thirty score and ten. Above all: are we happy about all of this, and can we stop it?

Either way, campaigning should be fun. At present Zoltan has a tiny team helping him, but he'll be launching a Kickstarter campaign in January to raise more funds. In the summer, he'll be touring California – his home state – on a campaign bus along with what he hopes will be a handful of six-foot-tall robots. Not everyone is happy though. There are those within the Transhumanist movement – many of them scientists – who don't like politics mixing with their pure research pursuits. Zoltan is a high-profile, but controversial, character within the movement – especially after his book The Transhumanist Wager, which is a philosophical near-future dystopian thriller in which Transhumanists manage to launch the third world war from their floating 'seastead'. 'The Transhumanist movement has a lot of older white males with egos,' he explains. 'But I'm representing a new part of the movement. Young, revolutionary, and political.' This has caused him some problems. 'Some of the older community are not very friendly to me,' he says, a little forlornly.

In the end, I suspect the Transhumanist Party, or something like it, will become part of the political furniture. It might take a little longer than Zoltan's hopeful projections, but technology and humanity's relationship with it is certainly changing fast, and will increasingly be an important part of political debate. That's usually a slow progression, but who knows? Sometimes political parties get thrust into the limelight because of events.

A human being killed because of the decision of a piece of artificial intelligence, for example, would certainly propel the party forward. Or perhaps something even more dramatic? 'If I got shot while campaigning in 2015 the party I could really rise to prominence quickly,', he says, almost hopefully. I couldn't tell if he was joking.

23 December 2014

⇨ The above information is reprinted with kind permission from *The Telegraph*. Please visit www.telegraph.co.uk for further information.

© Telegraph Media Group Limited 2015

Genetic engineering

Scientists can now alter the genetic code – the very blueprint of life. Some scientists claim that this holds great promise for the future of medical research. But is it true, and what does it mean for animals?

What are genes?

Every living thing has a genetic code in each of its cells, which determines how it will grow and what it will grow into. As a human being, you have approximately 20–25,000 genes, contained in the chromosomes, within the nucleus of every cell in your body. The genes are composed of DNA, which helps to build the proteins that construct and control the body. Different genes are responsible for physical characteristics such as hair and eye colour, and some genes are responsible for genetic defects, like cystic fibrosis. In most cases of genetic defects, individual genes do not cause such diseases. They are 'triggered' by environmental factors, and/or by the behaviour of other genes.

What is genetic engineering?

Animals have been used in experiments for decades in an attempt to find cures for diseases that affect people. This has led to a great many failures because animals' bodies are fundamentally different from ours. They don't get the same diseases as us and they often react very differently to drugs and chemicals.

Scientists are now using new genetic engineering technology in an attempt to create 'designer animals'. The aim is to 'model' in animals the diseases from which humans suffer. Genetic engineering is different from traditional selective breeding, where the organism's genes are manipulated indirectly.

The majority of genetically modified (GM) animals currently used in biomedical research are transgenics. There are two basic methods of creating these:

⇨ In knock-out animals, scientists have deleted, or disrupted the DNA in a gene, so that they can observe what happens when the gene fails to work.

⇨ Knock-in animals are used to study how a gene from one animal works in another. This is done by putting the foreign gene into a target animal and observing what happens.

There are now hundreds of different types of transgenic mice available commercially from catalogues or online. They are marketed just like any other piece of laboratory equipment.

How is it done?

In order to create a new strain of mice, young females are injected with powerful hormones to make them ovulate excessively. After mating, they are killed and the embryos extracted. The embryos are injected with the foreign DNA. These altered embryos are then surgically implanted into many surrogate mothers who have been hormone-injected to assist implantation and who will later be

killed just before or after giving birth. There is a massive failure rate in creating new transgenic animals: the vast majority (90–99%) of the offspring will not have incorporated the new gene and will be destroyed as 'failures'. For every successfully produced GM animal, hundreds die either in the womb, or soon after birth, or are killed as unwanted surplus. Even when the desired result is obtained, the GM animal will suffer additional side effects, as well as their designer disease, because the consequences of inserting new genes is so unpredictable. These unintended effects range from arthritis and heart disease to premature ageing.

GM animals in laboratories

Animals are genetically modified to mimic human illnesses, including asthma, diabetes, cancer, cystic fibrosis, heart disease, neurological (brain) disorders and many other conditions. But although the symptoms they display may appear to be similar to the human disease, these animal 'models' often react very differently, thus misleading scientists and slowing down medical progress.

For example, human cystic fibrosis patients suffer mainly from serious lung infections. Mice, however, have fewer mucus-secreting cells in their respiratory system. Therefore, lung disease is mild and infrequent in them – but up to 90 per cent fatal in humans. 'Cystic fibrosis mice', on the other hand, suffer from bowel disorders that are rare in people. Using GM animals in experiments produces results that are no more reliable than those obtained from ordinary animal experiments. Nevertheless, the use of GM animals in research is rocketing. The number of animals has more than trebled since 2000. Genetic engineering research accounted for nearly half of all animal experiments by 2012. The animals most commonly used for GM research are mice, but many scientists see primates as the ideal GM 'model'. ANDi, the world's first transgenic monkey, has already been produced in America.

Xenotransplantation

Genetic technology is now being used in an attempt to breed animals whose organs can be removed and transplanted into human beings suffering from liver, kidney, heart and other problems. Experiments have

been carried out in which genetically modified pigs have been used, and their 'humanised' organs have been inserted into 'normal' monkeys to see what happens. Such experiments have not only not worked, but have also caused enormous animal suffering. Putting animal organs into humans risks transferring deadly new diseases to people – for example, all pigs carry an HIV-type virus, as well as other potentially dangerous pathogens. There is also the problem of how to prevent rejection of the foreign organ once it is transplanted into the human donor.

Animal patents

GM technology is big business. One way that companies can make money is by patenting their 'inventions', which means that they have exclusive commercial rights over the new genetically modified animals they create. The first animal to be patented was the onco-mouse – in America in 1988. This very broad patent covered all mice genetically engineered to develop cancer. Many people strongly believe that it is morally wrong to patent living animals.

What you can do!

⇨ Join the Animal Aid youth group, and help to campaign against all animal experiments.

⇨ Find out more. Check out our website: www.animalaid.org.uk/ youth

⇨ Write to your MP and Euro-MP to voice your opinions about the use of animals in genetic engineering experiments.

⇨ Ask your teacher if someone from Animal Aid can come to your school to give a talk on animals in medical research.

⇨ The above information is reprinted with kind permission from Animal Aid. Please visit www.animalaid. org.uk for further information.

© Animal Aid 2015

Genetically modified monkeys created with cut-and-paste DNA

Breakthrough could help battle diseases such as Alzheimer's and Parkinson's but ethical concerns remain over animal testing.

By Ian Sample, science correspondent

Researchers have created genetically modified monkeys with a revolutionary new procedure that enables scientists to cut and paste DNA in living organisms.

The macaques are the first primates to have their genetic make-up altered with the powerful technology which many scientists believe will lead to a new era of genetic medicine.

The feat was applauded by some researchers who said it would help them to recreate devastating human diseases in monkeys, such as Alzheimer's and Parkinson's. The ability to alter DNA with such precision is already being investigated as a way to make people resistant to HIV.

But the breakthrough is controversial, with groups opposed to animal testing warning that it could drive a rise in the use of monkeys in research. One critic said that genetic engineering gave researchers 'almost limitless power to create sick animals'.

The work was carried out in a lab in China, where scientists said they had used a genome editing procedure, called CRISPR/Cas9, to manipulate two genes in fertilised monkey eggs before transferring them to surrogate mothers.

Writing in the journal _Cell_, the team from Nanjing Medical University reported the delivery of twin female long-tailed macaques, called Ningning and Mingming. Five surrogates miscarried and four more pregnancies are ongoing.

The CRISPR procedure has been welcomed by geneticists in labs around the world because of its enormous potential. Unlike standard gene therapy, CRISPR allows scientists to remove faulty genes from cells, or replace them with healthy ones. It can even correct single letter spelling mistakes in the DNA code.

The Chinese team, led by Jiahao Sha, said their work demonstrates how CRISPR could be used to create monkeys that carry genetic faults that lead to diseases in humans. But the same could be done to small pieces of human organs grown in the lab, and used to test drugs, or to monitor the progress of serious diseases.

Nelson Freimer, Director of the Center for Neurobehavioral Genetics at the University of California in Los Angeles, said that while researchers often use mice to study human diseases, brain disorders are particularly hard to recreate in the animals because their brains are so different.

'People have been looking for primate models for a whole list of diseases, but in the past it's been either completely unfeasible, or incredibly expensive. This is saying we can do this relatively inexpensively and quickly, and that is a major advance,' said Freimer.

But Freimer added that the use of monkeys was likely to remain a last resort. 'It's going to be really critical to define the problems for which this is used, just as you always do with animal research. You want to use all the alternatives before you propose animal research. This will be reserved for terrible diseases for which it offers hope that cannot be

gotten any other way,' he said.

Tipu Aziz, who has used primates in his work on Parkinson's disease at Oxford University, welcomed the new procedure. 'If we can identify genes for neurological disorders in a clinical setting and transpose those into a monkey it would be of massive benefit. I don't know that it'll lead to a rise in the use of monkeys, but it will lead to more focused studies,' he said.

Robin Lovell-Badge, head of genetics at the MRC's National Institute for Medical Research in London, said that genetically modified monkeys could be valuable to check new therapies before they are tried in humans. 'Mice are fantastic models for some aspects of human physiology, but they are not always perfect, and it's good to have alternatives,' he said. 'If you are trying to develop a stem cell therapy and want to graft cells back into the brain, it's difficult to know how it will work in a complex brain, and mice or rats are not suitable.' With CRISPR, scientists could perform far more subtle genetic tweaks than is possible with other methods, he added.

George Church, Professor of Genetics at Harvard University, has co-founded a company, Editas Medicine, that aims to use CRISPR to treat a number of human diseases. While monkeys had a role to play, he said another approach was to grow human 'organoids' or small clumps of human organ tissue in the lab, and use CRISPR to give them genetic faults that cause disease. 'This is a really big moment, because if you think something has a genetic component, you can prove it with CRISPR, and then improve it with CRISPR, or other therapies,' he said.

One idea in trials already uses genome editing to remove a gene

called CCR5 from human immune cells. Without the gene, the HIV virus cannot get into immune cells, so patients could be cured of the disease. In future, the same procedure could be used on healthy people at risk of the disease to make them resistant to infection.

Vicky Robinson, chief executive of National Centre for the Replacement, Refinement & Reduction of Animals in Research (NC3Rs), said: 'This research could drive an increase in the use of non-human primates worldwide. Whether that would be justified in terms of the benefits to scientific and medical research, let alone the ethical considerations, is open to debate. Just because the monkey has greater similarity to man than other animal species does not guarantee that it will be a better surrogate for studying human disease, a point that decision makers – funders and regulators – should take seriously.'

Troy Seidle, Director of Research and Toxicology at Humane Society International, called for an outright ban on the genetic manipulation of monkeys. 'You can't genetically manipulate a highly sentient non-human primate

without compromising its welfare, perhaps significantly. GM primates will be just as intelligent, just as sensitive to physical and psychological suffering as their non-GM counterparts, and our moral responsibility toward them is no less. In fact, the scope for animal suffering is increased because genetic engineering gives researchers almost limitless power to create sick animals with potentially devastating and disabling symptoms, which can include entirely unexpected phenotypic mutations. It's also worth noting that this research is being pioneered in China, where there are currently no laws or enforced ethical controls on animal experiments.'

Dr Andrew Bennett, a scientist with the Fund for the Replacement of Animals in Medical Experiments (Frame), added: 'Whilst the technological advances in genetic engineering are to be both applauded and admired, their subsequent use to produce genetically modified monkeys is questionable at best. Frame would call for more funding to be used to produce model systems based on human tissues and cells rather than try to develop more sophisticated laboratory animal species. If you're working on human disease, then it is necessary to use human-derived material to predict human responses.'

30 January 2014

⇨ The above information is reprinted with kind permission from *The Guardian*. Please visit www.theguardian.com for further information.

© 2015 Guardian News and Media Limited

100 billion animals don't lie: massive animal feeding review shows GM grain is as safe as any other

Whilst not attracting as much attention as genetically modified (GM) food ingredients, debate over GMOs in animal feed has long been simmering, and making sensationalist claims on the (allegedly negative) impact of GM feed on animal health is a favourite campaign tactic of anti-GM crusaders.

A new, peer-reviewed scientific analysis published by the University of California, Davis, *Journal of Animal Science*, 'Prevalence and impacts of genetically engineered feedstuffs on livestock populations', delivers yet another scientific blow to the anti-GM crusaders' claims.

In one of the most comprehensive analyses of published scientific papers on animals fed GM crops, the study concludes that GM feeds are safe, and finds that animals fed GM crops show no indication of adverse health effects.

The analysis adds to the considerable weight of studies that have been conducted into the safety of GM feeds over the years. However, this study is particularly significant due to size of the analysis. The authors, Alison Van Eenennaam, and A. E. Young, analysed data pertaining to more than 100 billion animals which had been fed large amounts of GM crops over the past 14 years.

Summarising publically-available datasets from the USDA of animal health and productivity, the author looked at data for the decade after 2000, a period in which billions of animals were fed diets containing large quantities of GM feeds, and compared it with data from prior to 1994, when GM crops were first introduced.

Deriving data from broilers (chicken), dairy cattle, beef cattle and swine which had been examined before and after slaughter by USDA inspectors and veterinarians, the study concludes that there was no evidence of reduced performance or increased adverse health in the animals that had been fed GM feed.

It's quite simple. If claims by anti-GM activists of tumours or animal mortality were true, it would be reasonable to conclude that this would be apparent to large animal producers that carefully monitor feed consumption and animal performance. Animals that are sick or stressed would have poor performance and feed efficiency (feed per gain). This study categorically proves otherwise.

Given that the anti-GMO activists are not prone to listening to the science, we're sure this study won't entirely quell their fear-mongering, but for those of us who prefer to make our decisions based on solid evidence, this is a very comprehensive analysis that puts to bed any doubts on the safety of GM animal feed.

15 September 2014

⇨ The above information is reprinted with kind permission from Monsanto. Please visit www.monsantoblog.eu for further information.

© *Monsanto 2014*

Our greatest challenge

By Philip Lymbery, Chief Executive of Compassion in World Farming

With the news today full of the latest scientific breakthrough in medical human cloning, I felt it a timely moment to touch on how so-called biotechnologies are offering new threats to farm animal welfare.

As important as our victories are in banning veal crates, sow stalls and barren battery cages, and with so much more left to be done generally to improve the lives of farmed animals and their transportation and slaughter, we have yet to face one of our greatest challenges.

In some respects, this imminent threat is not unlike those we have already successfully tackled.

Governments and farming interests persist in failing to address the fundamental problem of using animals intensively to produce food. Instead, they focus on the self-imposed problems they cause. Compassion must challenge simultaneously not only the institution of factory farming but also the attempts made by its defendants to 'manage' the animals' suffering. These measures, as welcome as they are, only go so far and not far enough.

The fundamental problem of using animals intensively to produce food does not go away just because some cages and crates can no longer be used. It has also got to be said that hard-fought victories like these would not have happened if we had not demanded them. History shows us that we cannot wait for governments and farming interests to always act compassionately toward the animals in their care. Or, indeed, in developing agricultural systems that produce humane, healthy and sustainable food for people.

This is the context in which I view our next major challenge – genetic engineering.

Farm animals are being genetically engineered for various purposes. This includes enhanced growth rates, increased disease resistance and altered meat and milk composition. Genetic engineering involves the insertion into an animal of genes from another species or extra genes from the same species. Alternatively, it can entail the manipulation, knocking-out or editing of an animal's own genes.

The genetic modification of farmed animals is hailed as the white hot, high-tech innovation to improve animal welfare and food production.

If only it were true. The reality is that GM can entail great animal suffering. Serious deformities of the cranium and jaw, feeding and breathing difficulties and reduced swimming abilities have been documented in some salmon genetically engineered for accelerated growth. What kind of technology is it that can impair the ability of fish to swim, to breathe, to feed?

Some GM purports to tackle problems that can be addressed in much simpler, less invasive ways.

Scientists have recently announced that they are to produce GM cattle without horns. Certainly the dehorning of cattle (a frequently performed mutilation) is immensely painful. However, it's not necessary to use GM to produce hornless cattle as conventional breeding methods could easily breed such animals.

> **'The reality is that GM can entail great animal suffering. Serious deformities of the cranium and jaw, feeding and breathing difficulties and reduced swimming abilities have been documented in some salmon genetically engineered for accelerated growth'**

There may be some very exceptional circumstances when genetic engineering may legitimately address animal welfare. Time will tell whether that will be the case. Certainly, we must be sceptical of any talk of GM being a 'benign way to help animal welfare'.

If we were concerned with GM crops, then, we should be even more concerned with GM animals. In the USA, the U.S. Food and Drug Administration is due shortly to make a decision on whether to allow salmon genetically engineered to grow much faster than normal to become the first GM animal food.

Our position is that, in light of its adverse impact on animal health and welfare, GM should not play any part in farming.

In particular, we call upon the European Union to prohibit the:

⇨ Genetic engineering of animals for food production

⇨ Use of GM animals and their offspring in the EU, which will make it pointless to import semen and embryos of GM animals

⇨ Sale of food from GM animals

⇨ Sale of food from the offspring of GM animals.

Visit www.ciwf.org.uk to read our four-page report entitled *Cloning and genetic engineering of animals for food production.*

16 May 2013

⇨ The above information is reprinted with kind permission from Philip Lymbery. Please visit www. philiplymbery.com for further information.

© *Philip Lymbery 2015*

Genetic engineering: synthetic milk may be next after synthetic meat

A plan to save the cows and make milk in the lab could ease the environmental footprint of the dairy industry.

By Jayalakshmi K

If the plans of a vegan duo materialise, cow's milk will soon be made minus the cow.

Genetically engineered yeast will churn out milk proteins in a liquid that tastes and feels like cow's milk.

Ryan Pandya and Perumal Gandhi who founded Muufri, a synthetic dairy start-up in San Francisco, started lab trials early this year and hope to have their synthetic cow's milk ready by early 2017.

The duo want to save cows from the harrowing trials of modern-day industrial farms that feed them growth hormones, artificially inseminate them and take away the calves to make the milk available for humans, they told *National Geographic*.

They plan to insert DNA sequences from cattle into yeast cells, grow the cultures at a controlled temperature and harvest milk proteins.

While the proteins will come from yeast, the fat will be extracted from vegetables. Minerals, like calcium and potassium, and sugars available in the market will be added to the brew.

They intend to use healthier fat than found in natural milk and a sugar more suited to people who are lactose intolerant.

Water makes up almost 87% of milk. Casein protein, whey proteins, fat, lactose (the milk carbohydrate), glucose and some trace elements make up the rest.

Not everyone is enthused by the idea or believes it will work.

'The 20 or so components of Muufri barely scratch the surface of milk's complex chemistry,' said Philip Tong, director of the Dairy Products Technology Center at Cal Poly in San Luis Obispo, California.

Others point out the high cost of extracting fats from vegetables, a process requiring water, fertiliser and high-quality farmland.

The debate on genetically modified foods will go on for some time as critics wonder how safe it is to ignore natural cycles and produce food in an engineered, industrial environment.

Perumal assures that his engineered yeast will at most produce a few animal proteins and die, in the case of escaping into the environment.

Muufri believes in fact that taking the pressure off cows and making milk synthetically will reduce the pressure on the environment.

As of 2006, 74% of the world's poultry, 43% of beef, 50% of pork and 68% of eggs were produced under intensive animal farming practices, according to the Worldwatch Institute.

These animal factories use artificial methods to maintain animal health and improve production, such as the use of antimicrobial agents, vitamin supplements and growth hormones.

It was just last year that Dutch scientists made a hamburger from meat grown in the lab and claimed the process could reduce the environmental footprint of meat production.

They grew bovine stem cells in a vat, turned them into tens of thousands of thin strips of beef muscle cells and mixed them with blood and artificially grown fat. Talk of the witches brew!

27 October 2014

⇨ The above information is reprinted with kind permission from IBTimes. Please visit www.ibtimes.co.uk for further information. Or view the original article at http://www.ibtimes.co.uk/genetic-engineering-synthetic-milk-may-be-next-after-synthetic-meat-1471878.

© 2015 IBTimes Co., Ltd.

Male-only gene trick could leave invasive fish species floundering

An article from The Conversation.

By Ron Thresher, Principal Investigator, CSIRO Marine and Atmospheric Research at CSIRO

THE CONVERSATION

A genetic modification that creates male-only populations could give us a new weapon against invasive fish such as carp that plague Australia's waterways.

'Daughterless technology', which works by removing females so a population can no longer breed, has previously been used to tackle mosquitoes. But new CSIRO research shows that it also works on fish.

The technology is safe and could be used to greatest effect with other forms of pest control. It might also be used to control other vertebrate pests such as cane toads.

'Rabbits of the river'

Invasive European carp have been fouling Australia's waterways and have been harming the native fish populations since they were first introduced to Australia in 1859 for aquaculture purposes. They became a major pest after the accidental release of a German strain, called Boolarra after the site at which it was being farmed, in the 1960s. They spread rapidly across Australia and quickly reached huge numbers, much like rabbits and cane toads before them.

Carp are now the most abundant large freshwater fish in some parts of Australia, including most of the Murray-Darling Basin. It is no wonder they are often referred to as Australia's 'river rabbits'.

So far, carp control has mainly involved commercial fishing or poisoning. While these options may reduce carp numbers, and poisoning may occasionally eradicate them from isolated areas, other options are being explored for more widespread control.

One notable success was at Lake Crescent in Tasmania, where carp were eradicated using a combination of control methods, including barrier mesh and traps to reduce breeding and capture the fish, and pesticides to kill unhatched embryos. The project also used high-tech tactics, such as 'Judas carp' implanted with radio transmitters to locate clusters of fish, and a pheromone 'lure' odour to attract and capture mature adults.

The daughterless technology being developed by CSIRO could be a useful weapon to add to this arsenal.

Testing on zebrafish

To find out if daughterless technology works on vertebrates, we tested it on zebrafish. We chose them because they are small, have a short generation time, and are closely related to several invasive carp species.

Daughterless technology involves modifying the genes of male fish. The modification is specific to a particular fish species, and there is an extremely low chance of it spreading to other species.

When the genetic change is inherited by female fish it reduces either their fertility or survival. The result is that females become more and more rare in the population, eventually driving the pest species to extinction.

In our trial, we managed to create a 100% male zebrafish population. Without any females, the group is doomed to die out.

Eradicating carp

The technology is now being tested on carp, at specialist facilities at Auburn University in Alabama.

Getting results will take longer than it did for zebrafish, as carp take more time to reach sexual maturity and the technology needs to be tested through several generations.

However, the preliminary results are promising – in fact it looks like it works even better in carp than in zebrafish.

This type of genetic modification has several advantages. The modified genes are spread through the population by the males, which are not themselves affected, and only through natural breeding events. As carp do not breed with any native Australian species, the risk of the technology affecting anything other than the targeted pest is extremely low.

Once our research is complete, our results will be evaluated by government regulatory bodies including the Office of the Gene Technology Regulator. We will also continue to consult widely with conservation groups, recreational anglers and resource managers, as we have done throughout our research.

Combining pest control

Daughterless technology alone can eradicate pests. But it is much more effective when combined with other control strategies, such as the use of pesticides, disruption of spawning activities, fishing, or the use of biological control (biocontrol) agents such as viruses.

In developing future plans for carp control, we could also learn from past successful biocontrol programmes for other vertebrates such as rabbits, which were brought under control with the aid of the myxomatosis virus.

CSIRO and the Invasive Animals Cooperative Research Centre are now investigating the Koi herpes virus (KHV), which could be a useful species-specific agent to target carp, and a valuable tool to use alongside the genetic technology.

KHV has affected carp populations in the United States, Israel, Europe and China. Having not yet presented in Australia, KHV may prove to be hugely effective if managed and implemented correctly.

Researchers at CSIRO's Australian Animal Health Laboratory are now testing KHV to ensure it will be safe and effective, before its possible release.

Rivers free from carp?

Can we look forward to a future where our rivers are free from carp, and many of our native fish are potentially returned from the brink of extinction?

That depends on research, careful and controlled field trials, consultation with the Australian public, and scrutiny by government bodies, particularly the Office of the Gene Technology Regulator.

Nonetheless, this research is an exciting step towards gaining the upper hand over carp and other pests.

CSIRO would like to acknowledge the funding agencies that have supported this research, including: Murray Darling Basin Authority, Lower Murray Catchment Management Authority, Auburn University, and the Invasive Animals Cooperative Research Centre.

8 May 2014

⇨ The above information is reprinted with kind permission from The Conversation. Please visit www.theconversation.com for further information.

© 2010–2015, The Conversation Trust (UK)

What will the world inherit from GE salmon?

Dr Gerry Goeden is a Malaysian-based marine ecologist, Research Fellow and Advisor to the National University of Malaysia, and marine consultant to the Andaman Resort, Langkawi.

By Dr Gerry Goeden

It's true; about 50% of the fish we eat are farmed. There is good reason for this as, one by one, the world's commercial fisheries collapse through overfishing. According to FAO (2010), 70% of the world's large commercial fisheries have either failed or are not far from it.

When things started to go wrong with world fisheries, fish farming was hailed as the ultimate solution. Fish could be produced cheaply and pressure removed from wild stocks. It seemed like the perfect solution to a very big problem.

Salmon are one of the world's most desirable fishes and incredibly predictable in their behaviour. Eggs are laid at high altitude in clear freshwater mountain streams. After a stay of up to three years the young salmon move out to the sea to mature. Most are caught when they return to the same river they hatched in, which they find by following a remarkable olfactory memory.

Early versions of fish farming followed an oceanic ranching model. Hatcheries produced salmon fry for release into rivers and allowed them to mature at sea. When the hatchery-produced salmon returned to spawn after one to five years at sea, they literally swam back into the factory that produced them, to become tomorrow's fresh fish. Ocean ranching still goes on but has declined or in some cases been halted due to low return rates and, more recently, regulation.

Farmed salmon differ from ocean ranched salmon in that they are not allowed to mature at sea. Instead they are kept and fed in offshore cages guaranteeing a better return rate and rapid growth.

Official FAO statistics report that commercial wild salmon catches have remained fairly steady since 1990 at about one million tonnes per year. This is in contrast to farmed salmon which has increased in the same period from about 0.6 million tonnes to well over two million tonnes.

This farm production of salmon is incredibly efficient and incredibly profitable. However, as lead researcher Professor Matt Gage from the University of East Anglia's School of Biological Sciences has said, 'Around 95% of all salmon in existence are farmed, and domestication has made them very different to wild populations' (Yeates et al., 2014). Which means that farmed salmon have the potential to genetically swamp the wild stocks.

On the face of it this didn't seem like a problem. Because salmon return to their original stream, each stream has its own genetic type or stock that has evolved to meet the specific conditions of that river system. Norway is home to the world's most varied wild salmon stocks, with genetically distinct groups found in the country's 452 different wild salmon rivers. But since 1971, Norwegian wild salmon stocks have diminished by roughly 80%. 10% of that country's salmon rivers have lost their populations entirely.

Explaining the crash of wild salmon populations

Back in 1971, aquaculture scientists started scouting 40 of Norway's best wild salmon rivers to find the ultimate genetic combination for farming. These 'designer' fish, selected for their ability to grow rapidly and use food efficiently, formed the breeding lines that by 2007 would, some ten salmon generations later, support a US$3 billion Norwegian industry. Salmon farming had become a machine for printing money.

The future seemed to be bright. Salmon stocks were flourishing and hatcheries were producing well over 170 million 'designer' salmon per year. But not all followed the rules. In 2007 alone, 450,000 Norwegian salmon escaped their destiny with the processing machines and this leakage of hatchery fish into wild stocks has been going on for 40 years. At the same time an estimated 470,000 wild Atlantic salmon were using the same rivers and breeding freely with the farmed strains.

In 2006, researchers Christian Roberge and Louis Bernatchez found evidence that farmed salmon had been evolving differently to wild stocks. These findings finally provided the necessary support for the suspicion that farm escapees could hybridise with wild fish and speed their decline (Roberge et al., 2006).

Many Norwegian rivers nowadays have as much as 50% hatchery salmon mixed into the returning catch. Because these hatchery fish are selected to grow faster, are aggressive, and are not as clever at avoiding predators as wild stocks, there is grave concern that interbreeding is reducing the fitness of wild salmon.

Jennifer Ford and Ransom Myers followed the survival of wild salmon in five regions around the world (Ford and Myers, 2008). They found that exposure to hatchery-bred populations greatly reduced their success. Wild populations experienced a reduction in abundance of more than 50%, seriously compromising their stocks.

In 2008, US Secretary of Commerce Carlos M. Gutierrez declared a commercial fishery failure for

the west coast salmon due to historically low numbers triggered by environmental conditions (National Oceanic and Atmospheric Administration, 2008). Hundreds of thousands of Chinook salmon (*Oncorhynchus tshawytscha*) typically return to the Sacramento River every year to spawn. At the time of the collapse, scientists estimate that fewer than 60,000 adult Chinook made it back to the Sacramento River. The fishery was closed until it could recover.

By 2012 and following the fishery failure, scientists had found that only about 10% of Chinook salmon spawning in California's Mokelumne River were wild stock. The wild fish had been 'over-run' by hungrier and faster growing hatchery fish and were now heading for extinction. Published in the journal *PLoS ONE* (Johnson et al., 2012), the study said that there were no longer enough wild fish to maintain the population.

A 2009 report from Oregon State University researchers found that steelhead trout (a close relative of salmon) were now so genetically impaired that they were unable to reproduce enough to survive (see Araki et al., 2007). It was only the huge hatchery output of young fish that kept 'topping-up' the stocks and giving the impression that all was well.

We have been flooding the rivers and oceans with voracious, fast growing fish that rob wild stocks of food and deplete their numbers. But the hatchery fish depend on us to make up for their weaknesses

and inability to maintain their own abundance.

This is fine for making money. But the day we close down a hatchery the salmon in that river may be lost forever. They aren't natural; like chickens, we have 'designed' them and they can no longer exist without our continuing involvement.

There may one day be a solution. A project carried out at the Norwegian School of Veterinary Science and the Institute of Marine Research looked at the use of sterile salmon in aquaculture to prevent the disastrous interbreeding of hatchery salmon and wild salmon. By producing triploid fish for the farms, escapees are thought to be rendered sterile. But disappointingly for the project, researchers found deformities and reduced temperature tolerance made the fish less suitable for farming. This solution is not just around the corner.

And now what's next for salmon?

The U.S. Food and Drug Administration (FDA) is reviewing the first genetically engineered (GE) animal for human consumption. And it's a salmon. Produced by AquaBounty, this transgenic fish adds genetic material from a pacific Chinook salmon and an eelpout (*Zoarces americanus*) to cause Atlantic salmon to greatly overproduce its own growth hormones. The new fish will grow two to six times faster during winter than wild stock and be ready to harvest at an earlier age.

By November 2013, Canada had announced that it would support the export of AquaBounty's GE eggs to Panama. The decision marked the first time any government had given the go-ahead to commercial-scale production involving a GE food animal. The FDA has yet to rule on the GE fish.

To date AquaBounty has spent about $60 million trying to coax the FDA and public into accepting their product. Within the last year, supermarket chains including Whole Foods, Kroger, Safeway, Aldi and Trader Joe's have said they will not stock the GE salmon.

What we must keep in mind is that this animal has never existed before; it is new to the planet; we made it. We really have no idea of what it will do when we lift it off the 'operating table'.

The FDA states that highly secure facilities will prevent GE salmon from escaping and affecting natural ecosystems. We are told that they won't be able to breed because they are all going to be females; each and every one of them. The GE salmon will also be made infertile, to prevent breeding with natural stock should some fish escape. (Actually it's reportedly 99.7% infertile which means thousands of breeding fish out of the millions produced.)

The future of the wild salmon stocks couldn't be bleaker. Norway is losing half a million 'designer' salmon a year from 'secure' farms, wild stocks in Europe and the US are collapsing, yet this new fish supposedly can't escape and even if it does, none of the millions of fish AquaBounty produces will interbreed with wild fish.

Craig Altier, a member of the FDA's Veterinary Medicine Advisory Committee and an associate professor at the College of Veterinary Medicine at Cornell University said, 'We need to treat these (GE) fish as we would a potentially dangerous medicine or pharmaceutical, and apply all of the same security measures to its production and transport.'[1]

Fredrik Sundström (1 September, 2009) at the Department of Zoology, University of Gothenburg, Sweden says, 'If transgenic fish become established in natural stocks they would be able to out-compete the natural breeds.' His work shows that AquaBounty fish would have a considerably greater impact on the natural environment than the hatchery-reared non-GE fish that are already wreaking havoc on wild stocks.

In itself, increasing the production of salmon is good for people and the economy. But it hasn't so far been good for the environment. Because we have decided not to let nature do the 'selecting', the salmon we have been breeding are weak and dependent. They pose a real threat to the existence of some of the world's most valuable fish. With the new AquaBounty GE salmon we will move further into uncharted waters; waters that soon may be filled only with salmon unable to exist without us.

References

Araki H, Cooper B, Blouin MS (2007) Genetic effects of captive breeding cause a rapid, cumulative fitness decline in the wild. *Science* 318, 100–103

Devlin RF et al. (2001) 'Growth of domesticated transgenic fish'. *Nature* 409, 781–782

FAO (2010) State of World Fisheries and Aquaculture (SOFIA) – SOFIA 2010. FAO Fisheries Department

Ford JS and Myers RA (2008) A global assessment of salmon aquaculture impacts on wild salmonids. *PLoS Biol.* 6(2):e33. DOI:10.1371/journal.pbio.0060033

Johnson RC et al. (2012). Managed Metapopulations: Do Salmon Hatchery 'Sources' Lead to In-River 'Sinks' in Conservation? *PLoS ONE*, 2012; 7 (2): e28880 DOI: 10.1371/journal.pone.0028880

National Oceanic and Atmospheric Administration (2 May 2008). 'Fishery failure declared for west coast salmon fishery.' ScienceDaily

Nebert DW et al. (2002) 'Use of Reporter Genes and Vertebrate DNA Motifs in Transgenic Zebrafish as Sentinels for Assessing Aquatic Pollution'. Environmental Health Perspectives 110(1): A15 | January 2002 [13]

Norwegian School of Veterinary Science (12 December 2013). 'Sterile salmon-reducing environmental impact of farm escapees.' ScienceDaily

Oregon State University (13 June 2009). 'Hatchery Fish May Hurt Efforts To Sustain Wild Salmon Runs.' ScienceDaily

Rahman MA et al. (2001) 'Growth and nutritional trials on transgenic Nile tilapia containing an exogenous fish growth hormone gene'. *Journal of Fish Biology* 59(1):62–78

Roberge, C. Einum, H. Guderley, L. Bernatchez (2006) Rapid parallel evolutionary changes of gene transcription profiles in farmed Atlantic salmon. *Molecular Ecology* 15: 9–20

Yeates SE et al. (2014) Assessing risks of invasion through gamete performance: farm Atlantic salmon sperm and eggs show equivalence in function, fertility, compatibility and competitiveness to wild Atlantic salmon. *Evolutionary Applications*, DOI:10.1111/eva. 12148

University of Gothenburg (1 September 2009). 'Risks Involved With Transgenic Fish.' ScienceDaily.

12 May 2014

⇨ The above information is reprinted with kind permission from Independent Science News. Please visit www.independentsciencenews.org for further information.

---

1. There are a number of other transgenic fish awaiting approval for commercial use including trout (Devlin RF et al., 2001), tilapia (Rahman MA et al., 2001), and zebrafish (Nebert DW et al., 2002).

© 2014 Independent Science News

Defeating dengue with GM mosquitoes

Dengue fever affects 100 million people, causes 20,000 deaths a year, and there's no known vaccine – but Oxford researchers are genetically modifying mosquitoes to eradicate it.

Dengue fever, which causes excruciating pain and death, is spread by the *Aedes aegypti* mosquito. Originally native to Africa, the insect spread throughout the world following the Second World War, and is now found in over 110 countries. As a result, incidence of dengue fever has risen 30-fold in the last 50 years, and now costs the world an estimated £3.5 billion annually.

Because no specific drug or vaccine exists, attempts to halt the disease's spread have relied – with little success – on pesticides and education to control the *Aedes aegypti* mosquito. Decades ago, US scientists began to produce sterilised male insects in the hope that their introduction to the wild would reduce the number of offspring and decrease the incidence of dengue. The theory was revolutionary, proving successful against some agricultural pest insects, but the radiation used to achieve sterility had adverse effects on mosquitoes.

Inspired by the concept, Professor Luke Alphey, from the Department of Zoology at the University of Oxford, developed a genetic modification technique which stymies the reproduction of the mosquitoes. In order to develop beyond larval stage, the offspring of Alphey's modified male mosquitoes require an antibiotic called tetracycline, which is impossible to obtain from natural sources in their habitat.

When released into the wild, these males mate with females and their offspring never develop into adults. The result is a targeted and gradual decline in the population of the *Aedes aegypti* species wherever it is introduced. The concept was patented in 1999, and then developed into a commercial spin out called Oxitec Ltd in 2002.

As with any GM technology, Oxitec has received criticism. But, unlike other GM products, these mosquitoes don't spread their genes down the family line or to other species. What's more, Oxitec is confident that, as an alien, invasive species in most dengue-endemic countries, their eradication does no harm to the ecosystem.

It's not just speculation, either. Oxitec has already conducted field trials in Brazil, Malaysia and the Cayman Islands with great success, in the process earning itself the title of BBSRC Innovator of the Year in 2009 and winning the Wellcome Trust Translational Award in 2011.

Now, plans are afoot to extend the trials. The long-term goal the company has set for itself is to reduce populations of disease-carrying mosquitoes by over 80% for as little as £3 per person per year in the areas in which the technique is used. If it can achieve that, dengue fever may well become a disease of the past.

Funded by: BBSRC and the Wellcome Trust

12 May 2014

⇨ The above information is reprinted with kind permission from the University of Oxford. Please visit www.ox.ac.uk for further information.

© *University of Oxford 2015*

Why are people paying for 'designer' dogs?

By Jody Thompson, Blogs Editor of The Huffington Post UK

One evening this week, I sat next to the most adorable little dog on the train home. He was such a cute, tiny scruff, almost smiling as he panted, sat on a cosmopolitan lady's expensive skirt-clad lap. Being a polite sort, I introduced myself to both pooch and proud owner and asked what kind of mix he was, before I stroked him (and got a dozen doggy licks as a reward).

Said owner looked me up and down and exclaimed, rather affronted:

'Actually, he's a Dorkie.'

I clearly looked confused. Haughtily, she explained: 'He's a Daschund-Yorkshire Terrier cross.'

Now it was my turn to look at her in a less than favourable manner. This has happened to me, a dog lover living in London, so many times over the past few years and it makes me so, so sad.

Saying hello to a dog and being told, it's not just a dog, it's the latest 'must-have' canine mash-up and the owner is the height of fashion for owning the latest breeding trend. People are paying hundreds if not thousands of pounds for 'Labradoodles' (labrador/poodle cross), 'Cockapoo' (cocker spaniel/poodle cross) 'Puggles' (pug/beagle cross) and 'Chorkies' (Chihuahua/Yorkie cross) and so it goes on, particularly in the tiny 'air dog' sorts.

Yet the vast majority of these dogs are bred by puppy farms with their cruelty and money-grabbing raison d'etre. Or else many of these babies are from unscrupulous breeders who show equally scant regard for animal welfare and no thought to the fact it is a terrible idea to cross for example, a Pomeranian and a Husky to get a Pomsky, both healthwise or behaviourally, which can only lead to problems down the line for the owner. They might sell themselves as 'family' breeders, but unless you see your prospective puppy happy and with its mum having a whale of a time in a home with its siblings, chances are the dog has not been bred ethically.

Yet a lot of new owners of the latest Labradoodles et al., whilst claiming to love animals, don't give the hard facts a second thought. Even if they have bought their designer dogs from a 'reliable' breeder, it begs the question, why even bother with a 'sort of dog'?! Why not just adopt a homeless four-legged-fella who just needs love more than most?

These owners sometimes come up with spurious justifications, like 'Labradoodles are better than normal dogs because they're hypoallergenic, that's why we simply 'had' to have one.' They're no more hypoallergenic than any other mutt. But having an on-trend, must-have dog is their only concern, whilst thousands of similar crossbreeds and pedigrees – who are not deemed fashionable – languish in animal rescue shelters in the UK, unloved and unwanted with some on death row.

Has Britain, famed as a nation of dog lovers, gone mad? Fashion dogs, gorgeous they may be (all permutations of pooch are, IMHO), but they are mongrels at the end of the day. According to vets I've spoken to for this blog post, they are not necessarily healthier than pedigree dogs either, especially those bred by reputable Kennel Club assured breeders who screen for diseases and possible hereditary conditions.

Don't even start with 'this breed/ that breed is better/nicer than this/ that/other'. Dogs are wonderful but can be unpredictable regardless of breed. My golden retriever Kim was

fantastic, but the least stereotypical golden retriever known to man. Ultimately you should only be considering what kind of dog on the whole will suit your lifestyle and whether you can look after it properly – mongrel or pedigree, big, small, needs lots of exercise, doesn't actually, etc. and whether it has been responsibly bred.

In addition, the latest Kennel Club research shows that 83% of 'designer dog' crossbreed owners receive no contract of sale and 81% receive no post-sales advice on caring for the dog. Another 84% do not have any health test certificates for the parents of their pups.

Another 85% were not grilled by the breeder about their suitability for dog ownership – so how many of these puppies will end up in rescue centres because the owner hasn't done their research and the breeder hasn't made them aware of whether the dog is right for them?

But still, people are thoughtlessly splashing the cash on what, in years gone by, would be common-or-garden crossbreeds, as fashion accessories – and feeding the hideous puppy farm industry. Yet unwanted, abandoned dogs – and some may well be Dorkies – are being put down. It beggars belief. You can't even use the argument that, well, a rescue dog could be a bit dodgy psychologically, as puppy farms and bad breeders don't concern themselves one jot in making your pup a well-socialised, happy baby.

There is a pet shop near where I live, and they always have moggy kittens and mixed breed puppies on sale for hundreds of pounds – the poor sad things, behind the glass, alone all day and often way too young for the recommended weaning age – and idiots buy them. It breaks my heart.

It also makes me furious because so many animals are so desperate right now to be adopted in shelters and these will be happier, healthier, better socialised animals. Buying from a pet shop simply justifies the animal farms and dodgy breeders to continue their cruel trade.

Every animal is beautiful, no matter what fashion dictates. I worked at a vets for years as a teen as I wanted to be a vet when I was younger, and saw dozens of unwanted dogs and cats put down as there was no room at rescue centres. The economic downturn has made matters even worse over recent years and the likes of Battersea Dogs and Cats Home, RSPCA, Cats Protection, Celia Hammond, etc. are overrun and desperately in need for people to give forever homes, donate funds, foster or volunteer to help the hundreds of thousands of unwanted and alone animals.

The phrase 'a dog is for life, not just for Christmas' still hasn't got through to some people either it seems.

People who buy a puppy (or kitten) for the sake of fashion probably shouldn't own an animal because they fundamentally don't understand what the responsibility is for looking after another living creature or what it means to adopt.

Let's stop this nonsense in 2014 and please, if you want a pet, why not forgo fashion and give a well-deserving rescue dog (or cat, or rabbit, or hamster) a chance? There are even pedigrees and perhaps some 'trendy' crossbreeds there! Believe me, anyone with any knowledge of animal welfare will think you are far cooler.

8 January 2014

Follow Jody Thompson on Twitter: www.twitter.com/ JodyThompson

⇨ The above information is reprinted with kind permission from The Huffington Post UK. Please visit www. huffingtonpost.co.uk for further information.

© 2015 AOL (UK) Limited

GM basics

Find out how genetic modification technology works and what it means for our food.

What is GM?

GM, which stands for 'genetic modification' or 'genetically modified', is the process of altering the genes of a plant, animal or micro-organism, or inserting a gene from another organism (living thing). Genes carry the instructions for all the characteristics that an organism inherits. They are made up of DNA (see an explanation of DNA below).

Genetic modification is achieved by altering DNA, or by introducing genetic material from one organism into another – either from a different variety of the same species or a different species altogether. For example, genes can be introduced from one plant to another plant, from a plant to an animal, or from a micro-organism to a plant. Transferring genes between plants and animals is a particular area of debate.

Sometimes the term 'biotechnology' is used to describe genetic modification. This can also have a wider meaning – that of using micro-organisms or biological techniques to process waste or produce useful compounds such as vaccines.

Why is genetic modification being used?

Genetic modification allows us to produce plants, animals and micro-organisms with specific qualities more accurately and efficiently than through traditional methods (some examples are given below). It also allows genes to be transferred from one species to another to develop characteristics that would be very difficult or impossible to achieve through traditional breeding.

People have been breeding animals and new varieties of plants for hundreds of years to develop or avoid certain qualities. Examples include racehorses that are bred to be faster and stronger, and roses that are farmed to give us a wider range of colours and to make them more resistant to disease.

Over many generations, and for thousands of years in some cases, the world's main food crops have been selected, crossed and bred to suit the conditions they are grown in and to make them tastier. For example, cattle are bred according to whether they are for beef or dairy production. Most of today's dairy cattle are very different from the cattle that were originally domesticated, as dairy herd breeding has focused on increasing yield and improving the quality of the milk.

However, whereas traditional methods involve mixing thousands of genes, genetic modification allows just one individual gene, or a small number of genes, to be inserted into a plant or animal to change it in a pre-determined way. Through genetic modification, genes can also be 'switched' on or off to change the way a plant or animal develops.

For example, herbicides are used to kill weeds in fields of crops but they can also affect the growth of the crops they are intended to protect. By using genetic modification, a gene with a particular characteristic, such as resistance to a specific herbicide, can be introduced into a crop plant. When that herbicide is sprayed on the field to kill the weeds, it will not hinder the growth of the crops.

Similarly, genetic modification can be used to reduce the amount of pesticide that is used by altering a plant's DNA so that it can resist particular insect pests. Genetic modification can be used to give crops immunity to plant viruses or to improve the nutritional value of a plant. In animals bred for food production, genetic modification could potentially increase how fast they grow and to what size.

What is DNA?

DNA stands for deoxyribonucleic acid. It is the genetic material contained in the cells of all living things and it carries the information that allows organisms to function, repair and reproduce themselves.

Every cell of a plant micro-organism (such as bacteria), animal and human contains many thousands of different genes, which are made of DNA. These genes determine the characteristics, or genetic make-up, of every living thing, including the food we eat. When we eat any food, we are eating the genes and breaking down the DNA present in that specific food.

DNA is made up of two separate strands of what are called 'nucleotides'. These are the building blocks of DNA and are twisted around each other in a double helix structure. The identity of a gene and the function it performs are determined by the number of nucleotides and the particular order in which they are strung together on chromosomes – this is known as the 'sequence' of the gene. Chromosomes are the cell structures that carry the DNA.

How does genetic modification work?

Genetic modification involves inserting or changing an organism's genes to produce a desired characteristic.

Inserting genes

Below is the process that takes place when a plant, for example, is modified by inserting a gene from another plant.

1. A plant that has the desired characteristic is identified.

2. The specific gene that produces this characteristic is located and cut out of the plant's DNA.

3. To insert the gene into the cells of the plant that is being modified, the gene needs to be attached to a carrier. A piece of bacterial DNA called a plasmid is joined to the gene to act as the carrier.

4. A type of switch, called a 'promoter', is also included with the gene and carrier. This helps make sure the gene works properly when it is inserted into the plant. Only a small number of cells in the plant being modified will actually take up the new gene. To find out which ones, the carrier package often also includes a marker gene to identify them.

5. The gene package is then inserted back into the bacterium, which is allowed to reproduce to create many copies of the gene package.

6. The gene packages are then transferred into the plant being modified. This is usually done in one of two ways.

   ⇨ It can be done by attaching them to tiny particles of gold or tungsten and firing them at high speed into the plant tissue. Gold or tungsten are used because they are chemically inert, which means they won't react with their surroundings.

   ⇨ It can be done by using a soil bacterium, called *Agrobacterium tumefaciens*, to take it in when it infects the plant tissue. The gene packages are put into *Agrobacterium tumefaciens*, which is modified to make sure it doesn't become active when it is taken into the new plant.

7. The plant tissue that has taken up the genes is then grown into full-size GM plants.

8. The GM plants are checked extensively to make sure that the new genes are present and are working as they should. This is done by growing the whole plants, allowing them to turn to seed, planting the seeds and growing the plant again, while monitoring the gene that has been inserted. This is repeated several times.

Altering genes

Genetic modification does not always involve moving a gene from one organism to another. Sometimes it means changing how a gene works by 'switching it off' to stop something happening. For example, the gene for softening a fruit could be switched off so that although the fruit ripens in the normal way, it will not soften as quickly. This can be useful because it means that damage is minimised during packing and transportation.

Controlling this gene 'switch' may also allow researchers to switch on modified genes, in particular parts of a plant, such as the leaves or roots. For example, the genes that give a plant resistance to a pest might only be switched on in the part of the plant that comes under attack, and not in the part used for food.

⇨ The above information is reprinted with kind permission from the Food Standards Agency. Please visit www.food.gov.uk for further information.

© Crown copyright 2015

Examples of labelling requirements under EC Regulation No. 1829/2003 for authorised GMOs (updated April 2008)

GM = genetically modified   GMM = genetically modified micro-organism

GMO type	Hypothetical examples	Labelling required?
GM plant	Chicory	Yes
GM seed	Maize seeds	Yes
GM food	Maize, soybean, tomato	Yes
Food produced from GMOs	Maize flour, highly refined soya oil, glucose syrup from maize starch	Yes
Food from animals fed GM animal feed	Meat, milk, eggs	No
Food produced with help from a GM enzyme	Cheese, bakery products produced with the help of amylase	No
Food additive/flavouring produced from GMOs	Highly filtered lecithin extracted from GM soybeans used in chocolate	Yes
Feed additive produced from a GMO	Vitamin B2 (Riboflavin)	No
GMM used as a food ingredient	Yeast extract	Yes
Alcoholic beverages which contain a GM ingredient	Wine with GM grapes	Yes
Products containing GM enzymes where the enzyme is acting as an additive or performing a technical function	N/A	Yes
GM feed	Maize	Yes
Feed produced from a GMO	Corn gluten feed, soybean meal	Yes

Source: Food Standards Agency, 30 January 2013, GM labelling

GM crops: timeline

Key events in the development of GM crops in the USA and attempts to introduce them to Britain and Europe.

1976

US company Monsanto launches its herbicide Roundup.

1980

US Supreme Court rules that genetically engineered micro-organisms are patentable. Spinks report recommends UK Government investment in biotechnology research.

1981

US Office of Technology Assessment recommends investment in developing GM crops, and predicts that salt-tolerant and nitrogen-fixing crops will be developed.

1983

First GM tobacco plant created.

1984

The First Framework Programme (1984–1987) introduces the long-term planning of research activities at an EU level.

1985

US Patent and Trademark Office (USPTO) decides that GM plants are patentable. GM crop field trials begin.

1987

The Single European Act explicitly gives the EC formal power in the fields of research and technology. UK National Seed Development Organisation and a large part of the Plant Breeding Institute sold to Unilever.

1988

First draft EC Directive on patenting biotechnological inventions is published, following a proposal from the World Intellectual Property Organization (WIPO).

1993

U.S. Food and Drug Administration adopts approvals process for GM foods, declaring them 'not inherently dangerous'. UK Government science White Paper: 'Realising our Potential'.

1994

In the UK, the Biotechnology and Biological Sciences Research Council (BBSRC) replaces the Agriculture and Food Research Council (AFRC). The first GM food, Zeneca's Flavr Savr GM tomato, appears on the market in the USA.

1995

UK Government 'Biotechnology Means Business' initiative.

1996

First commercial plantings of Monsanto's herbicide-tolerant GM soy in USA, engineered to be resistant to its own-brand herbicide Roundup. Flavr Savr GM tomato paste is sold, and then withdrawn, in the UK. Monsanto's Roundup Ready Soya is given import authorisation in the EU and the first shipments begin to arrive, where they are mixed, unlabelled with non-GM soy used in processed foods.

1997

Protests against GM soy imports begin in UK. Blair Government elected with financial support from leading biotech entrepreneurs and venture capitalists. Novartis' GM maize is given approval for import and cultivation in the EU. Austria and Luxembourg immediately ban it. New EU 'Novel Foods Regulation' comes into force meaning GM foods must be assessed for safety and labelled.

1998

EC Directive 98/44/EC on the 'Legal Protection of Biotechnological Inventions' is finally adopted, with support from the Blair Government, allowing gene patenting. UK Treasury identifies biotechnology as a key area for investment. Iceland becomes the first UK supermarket to ban GM ingredients from their own brand products. UK Government announces a voluntary agreement with industry not to grow GM crops commercially in the UK until a series of 'farm-scale trials' are carried out. Greece and France ban cultivation of some GM crops approved by the EU. UK field trials of GM oilseed rape and maize attract opposition.

1999

Five EU Member States – Denmark, France, Greece, Italy and Luxembourg – declare a *de facto* moratorium on GM crops until the EU Commission introduces legislation for traceability and labelling of GM crops and foods. US begins pressurising the EU, via the WTO, to break the moratorium. In Scotland, Professor Arpad Pusztai is sacked after raising health concerns about GM foods, following experiments in rats. UK Science minister Lord Sainsbury's report on 'biotechnology clusters'. DTI's 'Genome Valley' report claims high economic potential and strategic importance for biotechnology in the UK. Major UK supermarkets and food manufacturers begin removing GM ingredients from foods and products from shelves. UK farm-scale trials of three herbicide-tolerant GM crops (maize, oilseed rape and sugar beet) begin.

2000

Herbicide-resistant superweeds begin to be a problem for US farmers growing herbicide-tolerant GM crops. Germany, Austria and Italy ban several GM maize crops that have been approved by the EU. Starlink GM Maize – approved for use in the US only for animal consumption – is found in taco shells sold in the US.

2001

France, Austria, Finland, Luxembourg, Denmark, Italy, The Netherlands and Sweden all reject the Commission's plans to restart the GMO approval process, insisting that the traceability and labelling regulations must be in place before the moratorium is lifted. Blair gives a major speech on science to the Royal Society in London, attacking critics of GM crops.

2002

UK Government announces it will hold a public consultation exercise on GM crops, and produce reports on the science and economics.

2003

'GM Nation?' public consultation exercise in UK. USA, Argentina and Canada make a request to the Chairman of the WTO Dispute Settlement Body for consultations with the EU. President George Bush publicly attacks the EU's moratorium on GM crops and food. New EU regulations adopted, covering the authorisation, traceability and labelling of GM foods.

2004

Results of the farm-scale evaluations are published, showing harm to wildlife (due to changed herbicide use) for two crops (oilseed rape and sugar beet). UK Government approves GM maize for commercial growing but the company then withdraws. GM crops produced by Syngenta and Monsanto become the first approvals for import to the EU since 1998.

2005

Interim WTO ruling against the EU. Despite the interim ruling, the EU allows Austria, Luxembourg, Germany, France and Greece to maintain bans on GM varieties of oilseed rape and maize, imposed on public safety and environmental grounds.

2006

The WTO's Dispute Panel determines that Europe's moratorium on GM crop and food approvals between 1998–2004 contravened trade rules, on the grounds that the EU had not followed its own approvals process.

2007

Scottish Government adopts GM free policy. UK Government begins attempt to bring GM crops back to Britain. EU 'Plants for the Future' Technology Platform launched in collaboration with industry body EuropaBio to increase research funding for GM crops.

2008

UK press publishes repeated articles claiming GM crops are needed to 'feed the world'.

2009

The Welsh Assembly Government reiterates its commitment to maximising restrictions on cultivation of GM crops. Royal Society *Reaping the benefits* report calls for more research funding for agriculture, including GM crops, as part of the 'sustainable intensification' of agriculture. Food Standards Agency sets up a steering group to begin a new GM dialogue in the UK, at the request of the Prime Minister.

2010

European Commission approves BASF's 'Amflora' GM potato for commercial starch production (the first cultivation approval for 12 years). UK GM dialogue abandoned, following the resignation of two steering group members. EU begins to debate controversial new proposals to allow national bans on GM crops whilst speeding up GM crop approvals at a European level. Many member states object.

2011

EU allows low levels of unauthorised GM crops to enter in animal feed, with support from UK Government. Discussions over national bans on GM crops within the EU continue.

⇨ The above information is reprinted with kind permission from GeneWatch UK. Please visit www.genewatch.org for further information.

© GeneWatch UK 2015

The pros and cons of genetically modified organisms (GMOs)

Genetically modified organisms (more commonly called GMOs) are organisms or micro-organisms (i.e. plants and animals) whose genetic make-up have been manipulated by artificially inserting components of another organism. This can take the form of transgenic modification, whereby the organism contains DNA from another species, or cisgenic modification, whereby it contains DNA from a member of the same species but doesn't occur naturally. The latter form is generally viewed as a safer practice, although there are concerns for all types of genetic modification. However, the potential benefits of the practice are practically limitless, so it is imperative to know all of the facts about GMOs before making a judgement. Here are the pros and cons of such a practice:

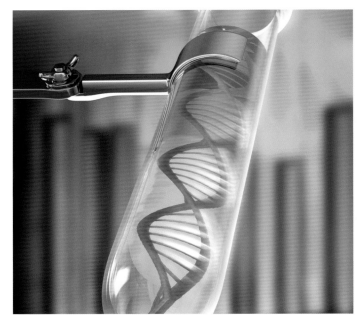

The pros

GMO practices can be used to produce 'designer' crops, which have more nutrients, grow quicker and produce more yield, are more resistant to pesticides and use less fertiliser.

Artificially implanting DNA from one species to another can save many, many years of research. Waiting for the unpredictable nature of traditional breeding methods can take decades to achieve the required equilibrium; such a goal can be reached instantaneously with GMO.

GMO experimentation can be used to manipulate animal (and, theoretically, human) cells to be healthier or desirable. For example, the article, 'Scientists One Step Closer to Male Contraceptive Pill' on the Labmate website, talks about how genetically modified mice are helping to research possible male contraception.

GMOs have been around for almost 20 years, so health concerns related to them should have become apparent by now.

Change (and specifically, unnatural change) can be good. For example, cleaning and cooking our food may not be natural but it is beneficial.

The cons

Studies have shown that genetically modified corn and soy fed to rats led to a higher risk of them developing liver and kidney problems. These health risks may not be transferable to humans, but they illustrate the unpredictable nature of GMOs on living things.

GMOs are not always tested thoroughly. The shortest GMO testing times are a mere 90 days, which many fear is simply not enough time to ascertain all of the risks.

Transgenic modification produces organism types which would never occur naturally, making them highly unpredictable.

GMOs could affect those with allergies in unpredictable ways.

Though GMOs were developed with a view to reducing the amount of pesticides used, this is not always the case. As weeds and bacteria become resistant to the pesticide, farmers actually use more, safe in the knowledge the crop will not be affected.

Often GMO products are not clearly labelled, meaning people do not have the choice to decide whether or not they wish to consume GMO products.

GMO testing often involves performing experiments upon animals, which some people feel is a breach of animal rights.

⇨ The above information is reprinted with kind permission from Labmate Online. Please visit www.labmate-online.com for further information.

© 2015 Labmate Online

UK laws regarding GM foods and labelling

By Mrs Green

Recently we were asked about GM foods.

Although I've signed petitions against these foods, because they just feel WRONG to me; I've never actually looked into the UK's policies concerning GMO food and labelling.

We were asked to investigate whether GMOs are accepted in this country and if they are, whether they have to be labelled...

I visited two sites – the Food Standards Agency and the UK Government site.

According to the Food Standards Agency, they recognise that some people will want to CHOOSE whether or not to buy GM food; which sounds hopeful.

The government site tells me GM crops are NOT being grown commercially in the UK, but imported GM commodities, especially soya, are being used mainly for animal feed, and in some food products. They go onto say: 'We'll ensure consumers are able to exercise choice through clear GM labelling rules and the provision of suitable information, and will listen to public views about the development and use of the technology.'

The Food Standards Agency say that any food in the EU which contains genetically modified organisms (GMOs), or contains ingredients produced from GMOs must be indicated on the label.

For GM products sold 'loose', information must be displayed immediately next to the food to indicate that it is GM.

However, they also say that products produced with GM technology (cheese produced with GM enzymes, for example) do not have to be labelled. I would have thought these products would come under the 'contains ingredients produced from GMOs' genre, but evidently not.

The most worrying thing is that products such as meat, milk and eggs from animals fed on GM animal feed DO NOT need to be labelled. I always advocate sourcing organic dairy, meat and eggs anyway, but this new information makes it even more important, in my opinion.

So here's what is currently labelled:

⇨ Any product in the EU containing more than 0.9% GMO must state the presence of GMOs on the label (apart from products derived from animals fed on GMOs of course – sigh)

⇨ GM plants and seeds

⇨ Food produced from GMOs

⇨ Food additive/flavouring produced from GMOs

⇨ GMM used as a food ingredient such as yeast extract

⇨ Alcoholic beverages which contain a GM ingredient.

And here is what is exempt from GM labelling:

⇨ Food from animals fed GM animal feed such as meat, milk and eggs

⇨ Food produced with help from a GM enzyme such as cheese or bread

⇨ Feed additive produced from a GMO such as vitamins.

If you want to avoid GM foods, then I would suggest the following:

⇨ Buy organic foods; at the moment organic products cannot contain GMOs. This is especially true for Soil Association certified, as they specify a threshold of 0.1% (the lowest detectable level possible).

⇨ Grow your own! Even if it's tomatoes, strawberries and salad, it's a start

⇨ Avoid some of the most likely GMO foods – corn, soy and rapeseed

⇨ Check out supermarket and supplier positions on GMOs

⇨ Buy meat that is labelled as exclusively grass fed

⇨ Ask the question – if something isn't labelled GM Free, ask questions because perhaps it is and they're just hoping you won't ask!

⇨ Look at the list of what is exempt from GM labelling and find alternative products.

I found something which I got very excited about – details of the four or five digit PLU code you see on fresh produce. It appeared that if the code started with an 8 it was GMO (and 9 indicates organic). However, it seems the addition of the '8' at the beginning of the code is voluntary at best, and maybe even urban legend at worst...

Ho hum; you win some, you lose some.

What about you – what's the GM policy in your country? And do you care about GM foods or are you happy to eat them?

4 February 2014

⇨ The above information is reprinted with kind permission from Little Green Blog. Please visit www.littlegreenblog.com for further information.

© *Little Green Blog 2014*

GM material in animal feed

Guidance on the assessment and authorisation of GM varieties for use in animal feed. Information on the source and quantities of GMOs imported for use in feed.

About this information

Applies in England, Wales, Northern Ireland and Scotland This information is for:

⇨ farmers and growers

⇨ importers

⇨ manufacturers and processors

⇨ retailers, caterers and carers.

Legal status

This is not a guide to either best practice or to compliance with the legislation.

Introduction

Before a genetically modified organism (GMO) can be marketed or grown in the European Union (EU), it must be authorised under Regulation (EC) No. 1829/2003 (this legislation is also known as the 'GM Food and Feed Regulation').

This requirement applies both to living GMOs, such as maize and soya, and to feed and food ingredients derived from the processing of GM crops. The authorisation procedure includes an assessment by the Panel on Genetically Modified Organisms of the European Food Safety

Authority (EFSA). The Panel assess the safety of the GMO and the food or feed derived from it. The Panel's scientific advice is then taken into account by the Commission and member states when deciding whether to authorise the GMO for use in the EU.

On the basis of these assessments, there is no reason to suppose that GM feed presents any more risk to farmed livestock than conventional feed. GM feed, which is very unlikely to contain viable GMOs, is digested by animals in the same way as conventional feed. Food from animals fed on authorised GM crops is considered to be as safe as food from animals fed on non-GM crops.

Transfer of GM material from feed

There have been some concerns that functional transgenes from GM-derived feed materials might be incorporated into livestock products for human consumption (milk, meat and eggs).

Biologically active genes and proteins are common constituents of food and feed, but digestion in both animals and humans is known to rapidly degrade their DNA, and the subsequent uptake of DNA fragments from the intestinal tract into the body is a normal physiological process.

In a statement published on 20 July 2007, the EFSA advised that 'a large number of experimental studies with livestock have shown that recombinant DNA fragments or proteins derived from GM plants have not been detected in tissues, fluids or edible products of farm animals like broilers, cattle, pigs or quails'. Broilers are chickens bred for meat production, and are not egg-laying hens.

When reviewing the issue later the same year, EFSA noted that 'the recombinant sequence is present in the GM plant only as a single or low copy number, which makes the potential absorption a rare event and therefore difficult to detect', and that 'when more studies are carried out with more sensitive detection methods, such recombinant DNA fragments may be more frequently found in the future'.

It is therefore possible that DNA fragments derived from GM plant materials may occasionally be detected in animal tissues, in the same way that DNA fragments derived from non-GM plant materials can be detected in these same tissues. EFSA also noted that 'no technique is currently available to enable a valid and reliable tracing of animal products (meat, milk, eggs) when the producer animals have been fed a diet incorporating GM plants'.

Authorisation of GMOs

Before the GM Food and Feed Regulation came into force, ten GM plant lines with potential use in animal feed had been licensed for commercialisation in the EU under the Directive 2001/18 on the deliberate release of GMOs into the environment (this legislation is also known as the 'Deliberate Release Directive').

There were also several products on the European market derived from plant lines which had not been authorised under this Directive because there had been no intention to commercialise the plants themselves in the EU. All were granted temporary authorisation under the GM Food and Feed Regulation pending their evaluation by EFSA and decisions on their continued use.

Temporary and full authorisations granted under the GM Food and Feed Regulation mean that, as at March 2013, there are 48 GMOs with a possible use in feed in the EU – 27 varieties of maize, eight varieties of cotton, seven varieties of soya bean, three varieties of oilseed rape, a sugar beet, and two micro-organisms. Apart from the micro-organisms, these varieties have been produced to exhibit resistance to certain herbicides or insect pests or in some cases both.

All of these GM varieties have been authorised for import and processing. Two of the maize varieties have also been licensed for cultivation, although only one is being grown commercially on a limited basis in the Czech Republic, Portugal, Romania, Slovakia and Spain. The seed is not marketed in the UK because it is not suitable for cultivation here.

A larger number of GM plant lines, including varieties of cotton, maize, oilseed rape, rice and soya bean which have not been authorised for use in the EU, have been approved for growing elsewhere in the world, particularly major commodity-exporting countries such as Argentina, Brazil, Canada, China, India and the USA.

In general, the EU's authorisation procedures for new GM varieties tend to be slower than those of other countries, a time-lag known as 'asynchronous authorisation'. To deal with the possible presence of unauthorised varieties in imports of commodity crops for feed use, the EU adopted a measure (Regulation (EC) No. 619/2011) setting a tolerance level of 0.1% for certain varieties for which a valid application for an EU authorisation has been made.

Labelling

Feed materials and compound feeds which contain GM or GM-derived material are required to be labelled to state as much. Labelling is not required for feed consignments containing adventitious or technically unavoidable traces of GM material, up to a threshold of 0.9% for GM varieties approved in the EU. According to the European Feed Manufacturers' Association (FEFAC), at least 85% (around 107 million tonnes) of the EU's compound feed production is now labelled to indicate that it contains GM or GM-derived material.

Supplies of GM material to the EU

The spread of biotechnology through commodity-exporting countries means that supplies of feed materials to the EU will contain a proportion of GM-derived products. It is not possible to quantify this as there is no legal requirement for importers to declare the quantities, but these imports are considered by the EU feed industry as unavoidable because the EU is not self-sufficient in protein-rich feed.

The European Feed Manufacturers' Association estimates that, annually, the EU feed industry imports more than 70% of its maize, soya and rapeseed requirements. Brazil, Argentina, Paraguay and the USA are major producers of soya beans and soya bean meal, almost all of which is now GM. Significant quantities of maize, in the form of distillers' dried grains and corn gluten feed, are imported from the USA; much of this will be GM. The USA also supplies the UK with GM sugar beet. The UK imports cotton meal from Brazil, India and China, and rapeseed meal from Canada; some of this is likely to be GM.

Identity preservation – this is the segregation of GM and non-GM crops after harvest and during transport, storage and subsequent use – is not routinely practised by commodity-exporting countries, but can be achieved at a premium. The additional price paid will vary according to the state of the commodity markets and the nature of demand for the end products (milk, meat and eggs for human consumption).

Quantities of GM feed materials grown worldwide

The area planted with GM crops has expanded greatly since the mid-1990s, from 1.7 million hectares in 1996 to 170.3 million hectares in 2012, grown by an estimated 17.3 million farmers. Developing countries account for 52% of this yield, although most of the farmers in these countries are producing on a smaller scale than their industrial-scale equivalents in the Americas.

The USA is the largest producer of GM commodity crops. In 2012, it had 69 million hectares under cultivation, followed by Brazil in second place with 36.6 million hectares and Argentina in third place with 23.9 million hectares. The other significant commodity crop exporting countries, each growing more than one million hectares of GM varieties, are Bolivia, Canada, China, India, Pakistan, Paraguay, South Africa and Uruguay.

The leading GM crop is soya, which by volume accounts for just under half of all the GM crops grown worldwide. GM maize is the second most common crop, accounting for a third of global GM production. Canada is the leading producer of GM oilseed rape. Brazil, India and China account for the bulk of GM cotton production. Overall, it is estimated that GM crops now occupy over 12% of the world's arable land, an area over six times the size of the UK.

2 July 2013

⇨ The above information is reprinted with kind permission from the Food Standards Agency. Please visit www.food.gov.uk for further information.

© Crown copyright 2015

Genetically modified crops could be planted in England this year

New legislation, which will be in place by spring, could mean that commercial GM crops including maize and oilseed rape are grown in Britain.

By Sarah Knapton, science editor

Genetically modified crops could be planted in England this year despite widespread opposition, following a landmark ruling in Europe.

The European Parliament approved a deal on Tuesday which will let countries decide for themselves whether they want to plant GM crops.

British scientists are firmly behind genetic modification, believing that it could help farmers produce plants which are healthier and need fewer pesticides.

The new legislation, which will be in place by spring, could mean that commercial GM crops including maize and oilseed rape are grown in Britain from this year.

In the short term, the crops are unlikely end up on our tables. They will be sold for animal feed, and so enter the food chain indirectly. However, it opens the door for genetically modified fruit and vegetables to be sold in British supermarkets.

However, a poll by YouGov last year found that 40 per cent of people believe that the Government should not be promoting the adoption of GM, while just 22 per cent believed that they should.

And campaigners fear that disrupting the natural DNA of a plant could affect biochemical pathways leading to the production of toxins which could be harmful to health.

Sally Beard, one of the founders of Mums Say No To GMOs said: 'Families throughout the country are not convinced by the assurances given by ministers and pro-GM researchers that there are no risks to our health and our environment.

'We have seen evidence of risk and can't understand why it is not being investigated rigorously and why GM production is not halted in the meantime.'

Friends of the Earth Senior food campaigner Clare Oxborrow added: 'Successive UK Governments have consistently championed GM crops and food – despite the fact that this technology has been hugely over-hyped and delivered little.'

Keith Taylor, Green MEP for South East England who voted against the new proposals, added: 'I remain convinced that GMOs cause contamination of crops, are bad for our health and that small scale sustainable agriculture is the answer to solving future food shortages.'

Under the new rules each European country will be allowed to decide for itself whether or not to grow GM, once it has been ruled safe by the European Food Safety Authority (EFSA), the EU's food safety body.

The deal has been engineered by the British Government who are fed up that GM trials continue to be blocked by Germany, France and Italy.

The ruling was welcomed by the science community who said that countries who refused to move towards genetically modified crops would become stuck 'in the Dark Ages of science'.

Professor Nigel Brown, President, Society for General Microbiology said: 'GM crops will help feed a growing population and require fewer herbicides and pesticides. I would have thought that was a desirable outcome.'

Crops are currently being trialled at Rothamsted Research, Hertfordshire and Norwich in Norfolk, but they will not be sold commercially. Wales and Scotland are opposed to the use of genetically modified crops and have already said that they will not be growing them.

Genetically modified crops are plants where the DNA has been modified to introduce a new trait such as the ability to withstand drought or insects. Scientists 'cut and paste' a gene from another organism with these capabilities and insert it into the genome of the plant.

They are already widely used in the US, Canada, Brazil, Argentina and India. Around 85 per cent of all corn crops in the US are now GM.

GM ingredients are already in food available on supermarket shelves, mostly in cooking oils containing GM soy or oilseed rape. However these will be labelled, according to EU law. Most supermarkets have banned GM ingredients in their own-brand products.

13 January 2015

⇨ The above information is reprinted with kind permission from *The Telegraph*. Please visit www.telegraph.co.uk for further information.

© *Telegraph Media Group Limited 2015*

Many in Britain still sceptical of GM foods

Four in ten British adults still hold negative views of genetically modified food, with few feeling more positively than they recall feeling 12 months ago.

By William Jordan, assistant editor

GM (genetic modification) technology might have prevented the Irish potato famine of 1845, new research suggests. Scientists recently announced that a genetically modified variety of Desiree potatoes has been developed that is resistant to late blight, the fungus responsible for the potato famine. However, a new poll by YouGov indicates that proponents have yet to convince a sceptical public of the technology's benefits.

Only 6% of the public report their views towards GM foods becoming 'more positive' over the last 12 months, virtually identical to the 5% who say their views have become more negative. And as for those whose views haven't changed at all, they remain decisively negative: 41% negative to 17% positive. A large proportion (31%) respond 'don't know' when asked how their views on GM have evolved.

Additionally, British adults say the Government should not be promoting the adoption of GM technology by a margin of almost two to one, or 40% to 22% in favour of such promotion.

In fact, the Government has shown support for GM and its adoption by British farmers. Environment secretary Owen Paterson said last June that GM foods are probably 'even safer' than conventional plants and food, adding that the Government and scientific community 'owe a duty to the British public to reassure them GM is a safe, proven and beneficial innovation'.

YouGov asked both questions in July 2013 and found roughly similar results, suggesting views really have not changed much nearly seven months after Mr Paterson called for increased adoption of the technology.

Currently GM foods are regulated by the EU. The crops are common in Britain, but are mainly used in animal feed.

21 February 2014

⇨ The above information is reprinted with kind permission from YouGov. Please visit www.yougov.co.uk for further information.

© YouGov 2014

Thinking about the last 12 months, have your views of GM foods become...

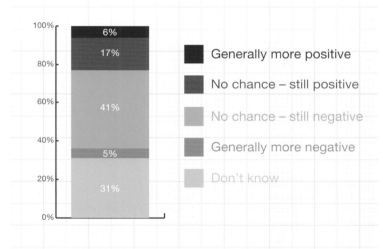

- Generally more positive
- No chance – still positive
- No chance – still negative
- Generally more negative
- Don't know

Do you think the Government should or should not be promoting the adoption of GM technology in the UK?

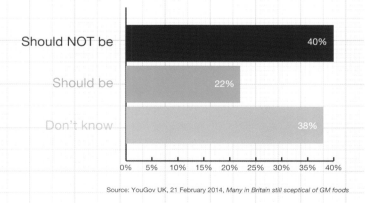

Source: YouGov UK, 21 February 2014, *Many in Britain still sceptical of GM foods*

Because we can, does it mean we should? The ethics of GM foods

An article from The Conversation.

By Christopher Mayes, Post-Doctoral Fellow in Bioethics at University of Sydney

THE CONVERSATION

Food is cultural, social and deeply personal, so it's no surprise that modifications to the way food is produced, distributed and consumed often lead to ethical debates.

Developments in the genetic modification (GM) of foods and crops has resulted in a raft of controversies.

Ethics can help here. While science determines whether we can safely modify the genetic make-up of certain organisms, ethics asks whether we should.

Ethics tries to move beyond factual statements about what is, to evaluative statements about the way we should act towards ourselves, each other and the environment we inhabit. But things are not always so clear-cut.

Three areas of ethics can help frame some of the concerns with GM food and crops: virtue, moral status and consequences.

Virtues vs vices

Ethics of GM foods can be developed by looking at virtue or character. Does the activity of engaging in the development of GM foods and crops erode virtues while producing vices? Or is GM technology a prudent use of knowledge for humanitarian goals?

Character or virtue-based arguments are seen in the case of golden rice – a rice strain modified to contain beta-carotene, a precursor of vitamin A.

According to the World Health Organization, more than 250 million preschool-age children are vitamin A deficient (VAD), and two million deaths and more than half a million cases of blindness are attributed to VAD. The developers of golden rice say it will supply 60% of the recommended daily intake of vitamin A.

But global outrage ensued after a group of Filipino farmers destroyed a test crop of golden rice. There has been little recognition of the Sisyphean struggle of farmers in countries such as the Philippines, Bangladesh and India, yet these farmers have been described as anti-science Luddites and contributing to the deaths of children.

Critics of golden rice such as Wendell Berry and Vandana Shiva argue that GM technology is a solution offered by industrial agriculture to address problems created by industrial agriculture.

Golden rice is a techno-scientific fix to structural problems created by some of the very companies that may profit from GM crops.

Although golden rice is a non-profit initiative, Shiva argues that it is a Trojan horse to give GM crops a humanitarian face.

According to opponents such as Shiva, golden rice and GM crops not only pose negative consequences for farmers, environment and the global poor, but represent vices of greed, arrogance and dominance. Rather than humbly working with and caring for the natural environment, industrial and technological interventions seek to master, profit and control.

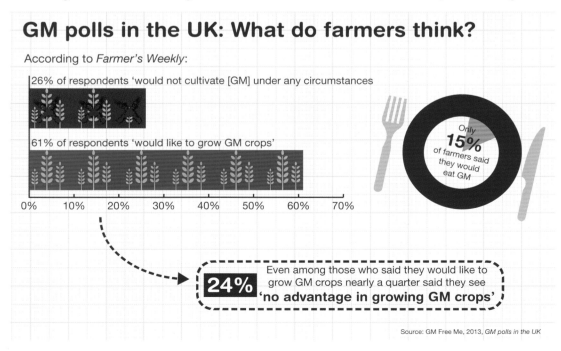

GM polls in the UK: What do farmers think?

According to *Farmer's Weekly*:

26% of respondents 'would not cultivate [GM] under any circumstances

61% of respondents 'would like to grow GM crops'

0%   10%   20%   30%   40%   50%   60%   70%

Only **15%** of farmers said they would eat GM

24% Even among those who said they would like to grow GM crops nearly a quarter said they see **'no advantage in growing GM crops'**

Source: GM Free Me, 2013, *GM polls in the UK*

Morality of nature

There are also concerns about the moral status of the organism itself – does the modification of an organism's genetic make-up represent a wrong to the dignity or integrity to the organism?

This position depends on arguments that nature has dignity and interests beyond those of its human inhabitants. Such arguments are not readily accepted due to their metaphysical or theological overtones and dependence on an essentialist idea of nature.

Appeals to nature can lead to what British philosopher G. E. Moore described as the naturalistic fallacy – the idea that we can derive moral statements from facts of nature. Examples include:

⇨ raw milk is good because it's natural

⇨ standing desks are good because we weren't meant to sit

⇨ genetically modified crops are wrong because they're unnatural.

Perhaps we aren't so concerned about the essential dignity of rice or wheat, but what about GM pigs that glow in the dark, featherless chickens, cows that produce human milk or the integrity of an ecosystem? Although the arguments are relatively the same, in discussing GM animals, the idea of a natural integrity or dignity seems more compelling.

Weighing up consequences

The most common way of framing the ethics of GM foods is to ask: do GM foods and crops present negative or harmful consequences for individuals, populations or the environment? Answers to this question vary according to context.

Most scientists argue that GM foods are safe to eat and will not harm consumer health.

While critics maintain that long-term health effects are uncertain, they contend that even if GM foods are safe to eat, other harmful consequences should be considered, such as the impact of patenting laws on farmers and research integrity, or the risk of GM crops contaminating other crops or escaping into the wild.

Debates over consequences tend to avoid the question of whether there is something inherently objectionable about GM foods and crops. So long as there is appropriate management of risks, then theoretically, there is no ethical problem.

It is unlikely these issues will be resolved any time soon – and likely that new ones will be added – but one area that can be worked on is discourse ethics.

Describing opponents of golden rice, even those that destroy test crops, as committing crimes against humanity or those in favour as pursing economic self-interest does little to move the debate forward.

Until productive discourse is established, barriers between opposing views will only strengthen.

26 June 2014

⇨ The above information is reprinted with kind permission from The Conversation. Please visit www.theconversation.com for further information.

© 2010–2015,
The Conversation Trust (UK)

Toxic crops

Most genetically modified (GM) crops fall into one of two categories. They are either engineered to resist chemical herbicides, or they are engineered to produce insecticides in the plants themselves. This means crops are designed either to tolerate specific broad-spectrum herbicides such as glyphosate or glufosinate, which kill the surrounding weeds, but leave the cultivated crop intact, or they produce a protein that is toxic for pests feeding on them.

Herbicide-resistant (HR) crops

GM herbicide-resistant crops have been grown commercially since the mid-1990s, mostly in North and South America. Cultivating herbicide-resistant crops promotes, and significantly increases, the use of chemical herbicides, such as Monsanto's 'Roundup' and Bayer's 'Liberty'.

However, over time, weeds develop resistances to the herbicides, which leads to the use of even more herbicides that are even more toxic.

This forces farmers onto an endless chemical treadmill. Weed resistance continues to increase, US farmers reported that on half of their land weeds are resistant to Roundup and that is spreading faster each year. Fields covered with resistant weeds increased by 25% in 2011 and 51% in 2012.

Pesticide-producing crops (Bt)

'Bt' crops are genetically modified to produce an insecticide *Bacillus thuringiensis* protein that is toxic for pests feeding on them. Bt crops produce this toxin in their leaves, roots and stems, killing insects like the European corn borer or rootworm borer. However, the toxin can also be damaging for other insects such as butterflies and moths, and the insect pollinators that conventional farmers rely upon.

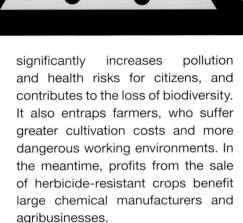

Monsanto's Bt maize, called MON810, is the only GM crop grown on a considerable scale in the EU, namely in Spain and Portugal. In Spain, contamination of organic maize crops by GM maize has caused severe hardship for organic farmers. MON810 has been banned in Austria, France, Germany, Greece, Hungary, Luxembourg and Poland.

There is still little known about how Bt plants interact with the environment. Very little research has been published about the various Bt toxins in GM maize plants and their potential effects on bees and other pollinators, and the impacts on soil ecosystems and organisms like earthworms or arthropods.

For the official approval of Monsanto's Bt maize, the impacts upon butterflies and moths are predicted using overly simplistic models that don't reflect the reality of farming methods and ecosystems in Europe, and the negative impacts are down-played.

To compound the unknown dangers, Bt crops are also constantly producing the toxin. While insecticides were traditionally sprayed at specific times to reduce insect populations, the Bt toxin is produced over many growing seasons and in all weather conditions – so that it is needlessly released even in years and periods where there is no pest threat. This contradicts the aim of current EU pesticide law that states that any kind of pesticide should only be used if the actual damage to crop yield from pests is significant.

The Bt approach to pest management is now considered a failure. In the US, reports state that Bt crops no longer provide protection against the very corn borers they were designed to resist.

Alternative solutions

The GM model of farming is unsustainable and damaging to the environment and rural communities. The increase in herbicides significantly increases pollution and health risks for citizens, and contributes to the loss of biodiversity. It also entraps farmers, who suffer greater cultivation costs and more dangerous working environments. In the meantime, profits from the sale of herbicide-resistant crops benefit large chemical manufacturers and agribusinesses.

In short, both herbicide-resistant and pesticide-producing GM crops are unwanted and unnecessary. There are currently no herbicide-resistant crops authorised for cultivation in Europe, and in several European regions, neither European corn borer nor rootworm borers cause any significant economic damage for farmers.

Experts agree: the most effective protection against the build-up of weeds and pests such as rootworm is to rotate crops and avoid monocultures where the same crop is planted year on year. Further protection against the corn borer is afforded by chopping the harvest left-overs and mixing them with the soil. Organic and conventional methods of pest prevention work – so why do we need GM?

⇨ The above information is reprinted with kind permission from Friends of the Earth Europe. Please visit www.stopthecrop.org for further information.

© *Friends of the Earth Europe 2015*

Does GM cotton lead to farmer suicide in India?

An article from The Conversation.

By Ian Plewis, Professor of Social Statistics at University of Manchester

THE CONVERSATION

Arguments surrounding the use of genetically modified crops and whether they are the solution to the world's problems of food supply and public health are no nearer to resolution than when GM was introduced.

In Europe, there is widespread opposition to GM crops, with import or cultivation of many GM foods prohibited by EU regulations. In the Americas, and to a lesser extent in Asia, regulations are less stringent and a substantial proportion of the area used to grow corn, soybean and cotton is planted with GM seeds.

The agri-business companies responsible for developing the seeds, notably Monsanto, are frequent targets of anti-GM campaigners. But not all GM crops come from the private sector, with considerable research underway at public research institutions or funded by charities – not that this provides protection from protesters, such as when golden rice field trials were destroyed in the Philippines last year.

GM seeds are not just used for foodstuffs. Most of the cotton grown in India comes from GM seeds, referred to as Bt cotton, having had the addition of genes from the *Bacillus thuringiensis* bacterium, which provides resistance to cotton bollworm. Even so, India has banned the use of GM food crops, notably aubergine, partly from the belief that the rate of suicide among farmers has increased in cotton-growing states since Bt cotton was introduced in 2002.

This belief was espoused by Prince Charles in 2008 and more recently by the controversial environmental campaigner Vandana Shiva. Anti-GM campaigns point to the costs of seeds and the fact that a crop failure can ruin farmers who then turn to suicide.

A look at the numbers

The suggestion that there is a suicide among Indian farmers every half an hour seems shocking. This is not a very helpful statistic however; there are more than 40 million Indian farmers in the nine main cotton-growing states.

Fortunately, suicide is rare, and no less rare among Indian farmers than among farmers in other parts of the world. In 2011, the annual suicide rate for Indian farmers in the main cotton-growing states was around 30 per 100,000 farmers. This is higher than in England and Wales where the rate is about 12 per 100,000, but similar to the best estimates of the rates in Scotland and France.

The evidence indicates that GM farming does not lead to higher suicide rates. In six out of the nine cotton-growing states, the suicide rate for males who did not work on farms was higher than for farmers. Also in 2001 (before Bt cotton was introduced), the suicide rate was 31.7 per 100,000 and in 2011 the corresponding estimate was 29.3 – only a minor difference.

The balance of evidence favours the argument that adopting Bt cotton has increased yields in all cotton-growing states except Punjab, and has reduced pesticide costs so that the crop has become more profitable for farmers. So it's reasonable to suppose that these farmers have reduced their debts and, to the extent that suicide has an economic component, are less at risk of committing suicide.

In fact, the available data does not support the view that farmer suicides have increased following the introduction of Bt cotton. Taking all states together, there is evidence to support the hypothesis that the reverse is true: male farmer suicide rates have actually declined after 2005 having been increasing before then.

The picture at the state level is less clear-cut, especially the contrast between Maharashtra and Punjab. In Maharashtra, farmer suicides have gone down, in Punjab they have gone up. Can we bring any more evidence to bear to understand this contrast better?

Unsupported trends

Both Punjab and Maharashtra have relatively high proportions of farmers growing cotton (26% and 20%) and Bt adoption rates are much the same. However, when we examine the effect of the introduction of Bt cotton on cotton yields, we find that yields have risen in Maharashtra but have gone down in Punjab. We cannot, of course, say that this is a causal effect but the results for these two states are in line with the hypothesis that there is an economic component to the explanation of suicides.

The Indian farmer suicide story has become received wisdom for some anti-GM campaigners. In fact, we find that the suicide rate for male Indian farmers is slightly lower than the non-farmer rate. And Indian suicide rates as a whole are not notably high in a global context. The pattern of changes in suicide rates over the last 15 years is consistent with a beneficial effect of Bt cotton, albeit not in every cotton-growing state.

The widespread adoption of Bt cotton – more than 90% by area in most states – means we will never have the opportunity to carry out a before and after epidemiological study of cotton farmers. Instead, we have to rely on official data at an aggregate level with all the caveats that entails. However, such a study might be possible if permission to grow GM vegetable crops is granted by the Indian Government (as it has been in Bangladesh) and might lead to a more definitive answer.

12 March 2014

⇨ The above information is reprinted with kind permission from The Conversation. Please visit www.theconversation.com for further information.

© 2010–2015,
The Conversation Trust (UK)

Key facts

- We have used the biological processes of microorganisms for more than 6,000 years to make useful food products, such as bread and cheese, and to preserve dairy products. (page 1)

- Three-quarters (75%) think that 'the Government should act in accordance with public concerns about science and technology'. (page 6)

- In February 2015, the House of Lords legalised three-parent babies. (page 10)

- Genetic engineering research accounted for nearly half of all animal experiments by 2012. (page 14)

- The macaques are the first primates to have their genetic make-up altered with the powerful technology which many scientists believe will lead to a new era of genetic medicine. (page 15)

- 'Daughterless technology', which works by removing females so a population can no longer breed, has previously been used to tackle mosquitoes. (page 20)

- Dengue fever affects 100 million people, causes 20,000 deaths a year, and there's no known vaccine – but Oxford researchers are genetically modifying mosquitoes to eradicate it. (page 24)

- The latest Kennel Club research shows that 83% of 'designer dog' crossbreed owners receive no contract of sale and 81% receive no post-sales advice on caring for the dog. Another 84% do not have any health test certificates for the parents of their pups. (page 25)

- In 1983 the first GM tobacco plant was created. (page 28)

- Any product in the EU containing more than 0.9% GMO must state the presence of GMOs on the label (apart from products derived from animals fed on GMOs. (page 31)

- Food from animals fed GM animal feed, such as meat, milk and eggs, are exempt from GM labelling. (page 31)

- Food produced with help from a GM enzyme, such as cheese or bread, is exempt from GM labelling. (page 31)

- Before a genetically modified organism (GMO) can be marketed or grown in the European Union (EU), it must be authorised under Regulation (EC) No. 1829/2003 (this legislation is also known as the 'GM Food and Feed Regulation'). (page 32)

- Temporary and full authorisations granted under the GM Food and Feed Regulation mean that, as at March 2013, there are 48 GMOs with a possible use in feed in the EU – 27 varieties of maize, eight varieties of cotton, seven varieties of soya bean, three varieties of oilseed rape, a sugar beet, and two micro-organisms. (page 33)

- A larger number of GM plant lines, including varieties of cotton, maize, oilseed rape, rice and soya bean which have not been authorised for use in the EU, have been approved for growing elsewhere in the world, particularly major commodity-exporting countries such as Argentina, Brazil, Canada, China, India and the USA. (page 33)

- The UK imports cotton meal from Brazil, India and China, and rapeseed meal from Canada; some of this is likely to be GM. (page 33)

- Quantities of GM feed materials grown worldwide: the area planted with GM crops has expanded greatly since the mid-1990s, from 1.7 million hectares in 1996 to 170.3 million hectares in 2012, grown by an estimated 17.3 million farmers. Developing countries account for 52% of this yield. (page 33)

- The USA is the largest producer of GM commodity crops. (page 33)

- The leading GM crop is soya, which by volume accounts for just under half of all the GM crops grown worldwide. GM maize is the second most common crop, accounting for a third of global GM production. (page 33)

- Overall, it is estimated that GM crops now occupy over 12% of the world's arable land, an area over six times the size of the UK. (page 33)

- OIn 2014, a poll by YouGov found that 40 per cent of people believe that the Government should not be promoting the adoption of GM, while just 22 per cent believed that they should. (page 34)

- According to the World Health Organization, more than 250 million preschool-age children are vitamin A deficient (VAD), and two million deaths and more than half a million cases of blindness are attributed to VAD. The developers of golden rice say it will supply 60% of the recommended daily intake of vitamin A. (page 36)

Biofuel

A gaseous, liquid or solid fuel derived from a biological source, e.g. ethanol, rapeseed oil. Some scientists claim that GM would be a useful tool in the quest to produce biofuels which would be beneficial for the environment.

Biotechnology

Biotechnology is the use of natural organisms and biological processes to change or manufacture products for human use. Biotechnology is widely used in modern society: for example, in agriculture, pharmaceuticals, the manufacturing industry, food production and forensics.

CRISPR

Pronounced 'crisper', CRISPR is short for Clustered Regularly Interspaced Short Palindromic Repeats and is a new technique for genetically modifying animals (a new way of modifying DNA which can reduce the need for breeding). In 2012, CRISPR was discovered in the primitive immune system of bacteria. It allowed researchers to create a break in the DNA helix at very specific places, where they can then introduce mutations as the break is repaired making it a much more precise technique. The precision offered by this technique offers an additional level of refinement for researchers – if they can produce better models for diseases then the results will be even more reliable. The technique is still in its infancy, but the potential for CRISPR is massive: it is cheaper, simpler, more reliable and requires fewer animals.

Cross-contamination

Sometimes, genetically modified material can be passed unintentionally between plant crops: this is called cross-contamination. It can result in the presence of GM substances in what is thought to be a GM-free crop, and is therefore one concern raised by consumers who want to be able to make informed choices about whether or not to eat GM food.

DNA

DNA (deoxyribonucleic acid) is the genetic coding which is present in every cell of living organisms. DNA is found in the nucleus of each cell and determines the characteristics for that organism.

Food Standards Agency

An independent government department set up to protect the public's health and consumer interests in relation to food. The Food Standards Agency is responsible for monitoring the marketing of products from cloned animals and their offspring, in conjunction with the relevant EU legislation.

Genes

A gene is an instruction and each of our cells contains tens of thousands of these instructions. In humans, these instructions work together to determine everything from our eye colour to our risk of heart disease. The reason we all have slightly different characteristics is that before we are born our parents' genes get shuffled about at random. The same principles apply to other animals and plants.

Genetic modification

May also be called modern biotechnology, gene technology, recombinant DNA technology or genetic engineering. Scientists are able to modify genes in order to produce different characteristics in an organism than it would have produced naturally. GM techniques allow specific genes to be transferred from one organism to another, including between non-related species. This technology might be used, for example, to produce plants which are more resistant to pesticides, which have a higher nutritional value or which produce a greater crop yield. Those in favour of GM say that this could bring real benefits to food producers and consumers. Those against GM feel it is risky as scientists do not have the knowledge to 'play God' with the food we eat.

GM food

GM (or genetically modified) foods are products which have undergone a process of genetic selection to produce a desired characteristic. For example, scientists may transfer the gene for disease resistance from one organism into a genetically unrelated crop, which would result in an improved yield from the modified crop.

In vitro meat

Animal flesh cells that have been grown in a laboratory and which have never been part of a living animal. Scientists are developing in vitro meat as a solution to the health and environmental problems associated with natural animal farming.

Nano-technology

The science of manipulating atoms and/or molecules to create materials and devices. This is all done on an extremely small scale – a nanometer is one billionth of a meter. Examples of nano-technology includes micro-electronics (think tiny computer chips) and also nano-machines (incredibly small machines such as gears, switches etc. or even nano-robots).

Selective breeding

Human beings have been modifying the genes of biological organisms for centuries through selective breeding: choosing individual plants and animals with particular traits, like fast growth rates or good seed production, and breeding them with others to produce the most desirable combination of characteristics. However, unlike genetic modification, this can happen only within closely-related species.

Synthetic biology

Synthetic biology (synbio) is an extreme version of genetic engineering. Instead of swapping genes from one species to another (as in conventional genetic engineering), synthetic biologists employ a number of new genetic engineering techniques, such as using synthetic (human-made) DNA to create entirely new forms of life or to 'reprogramme' existing organisms to produce chemicals that they would not produce naturally.

Assignments

Brainstorming

⇨ In small groups, discuss what you know about biotechnology. Consider the following questions:

- What is biotechnology?
- What do you think of when you hear the term 'biotechnology'?

⇨ In groups, create two spider diagrams on A2 paper. One should include all the reasons you can think of to support the idea of using biotechnology to develop synthetic food such as meat and milk, whilst the other should present the arguments against it. Which diagram is more convincing? Feedback to your class and discuss the points on your diagrams.

Research

⇨ Create a questionnaire that will explore opinions about GM crops. You should aim to find out:

- How much people know about Genetic Modification of crops (and how this varies between age groups).
- Whether people view GM positively or negatively.

Analyse your results and write a report that includes at least two graphs/visual representations of your data.

⇨ Read through some recent news stories about biotechnology or genetic modification. Choose a story that peaks your interest and conduct further research. Make notes and present them to your class in a quick two-minute presentation. Look at the 'useful weblinks' at the front of this book, or visit Issues Online for help with your research.

⇨ Choose a point on the GM crops timeline, page 28, and research it further. Write a short summary of your findings.

⇨ Read the article *Genetically modified crops could be planted in England this year* and research the validity of the article. Write some notes and feedback to your class, considering whether you think the author was objective/accurate.

Design

⇨ Imagine that you work for a company who have created a synthetic meat that tastes like chicken. Think of a name and a logo for your new product then design a poster and some sample pages from your company website. You could even suggest some recipes for people to try. Get creative! (Work in groups or pairs.)

⇨ Imagine that you are campaigning for the Transhumanist party. Design and leaflet and poster that will explain the ethos of the party.

⇨ Choose an illustration from this book and write a paragraph exploring what the artist was trying to portray with his image.

Oral

⇨ 'Genetic modification that is used to create medicines is more ethically justifiable than genetic modification used to adapt or create food.' In small groups, discuss your feelings and opinions about this statement. Write some notes then nominate one person to feedback your different ideas to the rest of the class.

⇨ 'Genetic modification should be illegal, no matter what it is used for.' Stage a class-debate in which half of you argue in favour of the statement and half of your argue against it.

⇨ Imagine you are a part of a research team which is trying to introduce *in vitro* meat into supermarkets. In groups of four, create a TV advert which informs viewers of the benefits of lab-grown meat compared to farmed animal meat. You will need to reassure consumers of the safety of the product and make it sound appealing. Consider how you could encourage consumers to try the product while addressing any fears they may have.

⇨ 'A. E. Young analysed data pertaining to more than 100 billion animals which had been fed large amounts of GM crops over the past 14 years... the study concludes that there was no evidence of reduced performance or increased adverse health in the animals that had been fed GM feed.' (Source: *100 billion animals don't lie: massive animal feeding review shows GM grain is as safe as any other*, page 17). In pairs, read the article this quote was taken from and consider whether this research was objective. Think about the source of the article and do some further research into the study mentioned above. Write some notes on your findings and feedback to your class.

Reading/writing

⇨ Write a blog post from the point of view of a scientist who is developing synthetic milk. Write about the things you hope to achieve with this development.

⇨ Watch the film *Rise of the Planet of the Apes* (2011) and write a review discussing how the director addresses the theme of biotechnology.

⇨ Read the article *The pros and cons of genetically modified organisms (GMOs)* and write a summary for your school newspaper, adding in your own opinions if you feel it is necessary.

Acknowledgements

The publisher is grateful for permission to reproduce the material in this book. While every care has been taken to trace and acknowledge copyright, the publisher tenders its apology for any accidental infringement or where copyright has proved untraceable. The publisher would be pleased to come to a suitable arrangement in any such case with the rightful owner.

Images

All images courtesy of iStock, except page 14 © Nick Saltmarsh, page 19 © Benjamin Horn, page 22 © Julia Manzerova, page 32 © A J Garrison and page 37 © Andrew Gustar.

Icons on page 6 are reproduced courtesy of Freepik.

Illustrations

Don Hatcher: pages 5 & 16. Simon Kneebone: pages 12 & 29. Angelo Madrid: pages 8 & 13.

Additional acknowledgements

Editorial on behalf of Independence Educational Publishers by Cara Acred.

With thanks to the Independence team: Mary Chapman, Sandra Dennis, Christina Hughes, Jackie Staines and Jan Sunderland.

Cara Acred

Cambridge

May 2015